TWELVE·
TRIBE
NATIONS
and
the Science of
Enchanting the
Landscape

TWELVE-TRIBE NATIONS

NATIONS

and
the Science of
Enchanting the
Landscape

JOHN MICHELL
and
CHRISTINE RHONE

with 84 illustrations

THAMES AND HUDSON

Designed by Liz Rudderham

Printed and bound in Yugoslavia

Contents

Contents

Introduction:
the Grail, what it is
and where to look for it

Modern civilization has many advantages, but it does not seem very stable, and it has obviously not been designed for long endurance. It is fascinating therefore to look back on ancient societies, when the main priority was permanence, and rulers were chiefly concerned with keeping up the inherited religion, culture and customs of their tribe or nation. The common experience of life in one of the traditional societies of the past was clearly different from that which is produced by modern conditions. Every age knows grief and tragedy, and there was probably more physical hardship in the past than most of us have to endure today. Yet the more one learns about life in the ancient world, the more one becomes aware of a quality which is absent from our own, though it is still commonly experienced in childhood: a quality of enchantment.

An enchantment is something that takes hold of the individual or collective imagination. We cannot enter into past minds, but we can to some extent know what chiefly affected them, the world-view, mythology, religious allegories, ritual and music which prevailed in their times. Through these we can gain some impression of how the ancient world appeared to those who lived in it. It was a world in which gods and ancestral spirits constantly intervened in human affairs and animated every landscape, where mundane and spiritual life were closely interwoven.

Existence in those conditions had an intensity which is reflected in all the traditions and relics of antiquity. We detect it in the old myths and local legends, in ancient religious chants and folksongs and in the harmonious proportions of temples throughout the world, perfectly adapted to the spiritual character of their surroundings. All these in every nation were products of a unified culture and a ruling priesthood which upheld it. We can speak cynically about the arts of priestcraft and how they were used to beguile and exploit the populace; but that is just one side of the picture. Those arts were used not only to gain political and economic control, but also, on a more subtle level, to create and maintain a certain level of illusion – in other words, to form the reality which people experienced. Thus we speak of enchantment. There are many different kinds of enchantments, both good and evil, and history gives examples of the two extremes. But the form of enchantment which we are here investigating stands apart from all others, because in many countries and at many different periods it has been recognized as the form most conducive to human happiness and freedom within the confines of an ordered, settled community.

In searching for the secrets of ancient enchantment we are in effect seeking the Grail, for the Grail legend is of a former enchantment, now broken, which will one day be restored. One day the lost Grail will be found again. It is a vessel which gives nourishment. It heals a sick people and transforms their disenchanted country, the wasteland, back into its natural, primeval character as the terrestrial paradise.

The legend of the Grail is the Celtic version, with particular application to Britain, of a universal theme concerning something which has vanished and must be found or invoked again for the redemption of life on earth. To Hindus the Grail quest is for Soma, the drink of immortality. The Jews dream of reconstructing the perfectly proportioned Temple of Jerusalem, and this ideal has been adopted by a succession of esoteric Christian groups, such as the Knights Templar, and also by the freemasons. With the rebuilding of the Temple is prophesied the gathering at Jerusalem of the twelve tribes of Israel, ten of which are at present 'scattered among the nations of the world'. This will set in motion the millennial process leading to the renewal of divine governance.

In all the many such legends and prophecies, the lost sources of regeneration, though variously symbolized, have the same archetypal reference. They indicate something – an object, method or medium – which causes life to be experienced on its highest, most heroic level, while giving to human nature what it most requires: to express itself freely, within a just, well-ordered but high-spirited society. Where this ideal is realized, there surely is paradise on earth.

The quest for the Grail begins with the question of what exactly one is looking for. Whatever it may be, it is something which has an immediate, dramatic, widespread effect whenever it is rediscovered. People's minds are stunned into a new way of thinking, and the change is reflected in a new, idealistic form of society. Yet, besides creating a sensation, it has a further, long-lasting quality. It serves as a constant fount of inspiration and wisdom, sanctifying the lives of those who possess it. When it is lost, harmony and good order vanish with it.

The circumstances in which the Grail is revealed are unpredictable and must await their time. Its contents, however, can reasonably be identified. A hint is given in René Guénon's book, *Le Roi du monde*, where he remarks on the similarity between the word *grasale*, a grail or vessel, and *gradale* or *graduale*, a book. The vessel contains the inspiring potion which returns whoever drinks it to the state of primordial vision. The book signifies the primordial tradition. These two things are inseparable in constituting the full meaning of the Grail, either one of them being ineffectual without the other.

The primordial vision refers to that not uncommon type of experience, sought by mystics and often occurring spontaneously to ordinary people, where in a sudden moment of transcendence one glimpses a world of far higher beauty and significance than that of normal perception, and has a feeling of total harmony with it. Much has been written about that experience, and many who have once known it have devoted lifetimes to regaining it, by methods ranging from asceticism to debauchery.

The vision is called primordial because it is likely to have been achieved more commonly in times before civilization, when human perception was necessarily sharper and more intuitive. Under its spell, one enters briefly into that lost world of enchantment which is hinted at in the arts and artefacts of antiquity and is described poetically in the legend of the Grail.

In modern society such visions serve no recognized function and can therefore prove maddening and destructive. With no available source of guidance, the opened mind is prone to obsession by fantasies and superstitions. The traditional remedy is that applied by the shamans of tribal societies where visionary experience is respected and valued. It consists in education. The visionary is initiated into the esoteric lore of the tribe and is marked out as a potential shaman or wise elder. His vision is not suppressed but made use of.

Thus are united the two sides of that whole which is symbolized by the Grail. With the primordial vision goes the primordial tradition. The first without the second provides a fleeting sensation of no lasting benefit; the second on its own is lifeless and without purpose. Together they may bring about the state of mind and perception which is appropriate to a golden age.

If one speaks today in general society about the primordial tradition one is likely to meet a blank response. The Grail is indeed lost, and probably has never been more deeply buried than at the present time, when the existence of such a tradition is unknown to, or ignored by, those who have charge of education. Material progress and inventiveness being the modern requirements, there seems nothing to be gained by studying the traditional form of knowledge which produced the philosophy and science of ancient times.

The tradition whose rediscovery is associated with the Grail (and with all periods of cultural renaissance) is essentially a cosmology or model of the universe. Plato refers to it in the *Laws* (656) as a canon of sacred music. By control of music, he says, and by licensing only such compositions as create harmony in the soul and in society, the ancient Egyptians preserved their civilization from corruption for ten thousand years. In the first instance the canon was a code of number, from which were derived the psychologically beneficial types of music and the geometric and architectural proportions which are most appealing to the aesthetic eye. The ancient philosophers understood the structure of number to be analogous with the structure of creation, and they realized also that number is basically duodecimal, being naturally governed by the number twelve. By reference to their sacred canon of number, they ordered their societies and all their institutions within a duodecimal framework. Through their science, and by constant vigilance against the corruption of its standards, they cast a spell over whole countries and spread a golden-age air of enchantment across many generations.

I

The universal twelve tribes

All over the world, in countries as far apart as China, Peru, Iceland and Madagascar, are records and traditions of whole nations and their territories being divided into twelve tribes and twelve regions, each tribe and its sector of land corresponding to one of the twelve signs of the zodiac and to one of the twelve months in the year. Other periods of time were symbolized in these societies by prior divisions of the tribes into two groups to represent night and day, and into four sections with three tribes to each, in imitation of the four seasons and the four points of the compass. A formal state cosmology provided the model for such organizations. It was numerically framed and based on the number twelve (or, for brevity and emphasis, 12). It regulated every aspect of life from religious and state ritual to the arrangements of clans, villages and families.

Each tribe was ruled by a chief or king whose dynasty was traditionally founded by the god of their region, and in each group of three one of the kings was superior to the others and ruled over that quarter. The same hierarchical pattern was repeated throughout, down to individual households, so that the structure of every unit in society reflected that of the state itself.

The 12 tribes each had their own customs and assemblies, but were united by a common religion, culture and code of law. Together they formed a zodiacal wheel, at the hub of which was a sacred mountain, mound or acropolis rock which represented the pole of their universe. Around it lay the national sanctuary, symbolically designed as an image of paradise, and there the 12 tribes came together every year for ceremonies and festivals under a high king whose authority was equivalent to that of the sun as ruler of the heavens. In some societies the office of high king was hereditary or filled by election, while in others it was held by each of the 12 tribal kings in turn.

The foundation plan of these 12-tribe societies was a symbolic chart of the heavens, divided into 12 sectors which were named after 12 constellations and governed by 12 principal gods. It is impossible to say when or where this idea arose, for it occurs in the earliest traditions and histories of virtually every nation. Systems of 12 gods, corresponding to the division of the year into 12 months and of the heavens into 12 astrological houses, were adopted in ancient Egypt, Phoenicia, Chaldaea, Persia and throughout the East. The 12 Babylonian gods, according to Diodorus Siculus, ruled the 12 signs of the zodiac and were each worshipped in the appropriate month. Similarly in Greece, Hesiod's creation myth names 12 primordial gods, born of heaven and earth, six
1b male (the Titans) and six female. Zeus on Mount Olympus presided
1a over a 12-god pantheon, and statues of 12 gods stood in the Forum at Rome. At Asgard, the Nordic Olympus, Odin sat enthroned amid 12 divine councillors. The Hindus from the time of the Brahmanas have recognized 12 solar gods, the Adityas, each representing a twelfth part of the sun's progress through the zodiac, and Brahma employed 12 Jayas to help him fashion the world. In the Japanese Shinto cosmogony 12 Kami correspond to 12 stages in creation, and in the Zoroastrian *Bundahish* 12 Akhtars, representing the 12 zodiacal signs, led the army of Ormazd.

On the principle, as above so below, every nation that acknowledged 12 gods, constellations and signs of the zodiac arranged its society and landscape accordingly. Thus the Emperor Yao, who presided over a legendary golden age in China at the beginning of the third millennium BC, divided his realm astrologically, first into four quarters and then into 12 regions governed by 12 mandarins. Even earlier, in the fourth millennium BC, the Sumerians knew the 12-sign zodiac and the 360-degree circle and made a 12-part division of their territory. The old Vedic kings were advised by a court of 12 nobles whose houses they visited during their 12-day period of
2 consecration, and in Tibet the Dalai Lama ruled through a circular council of 12 elders. In the great days of Israel, 12 princes administered the 12-tribe kingdom of King Solomon.

The 12-fold structure of theologies, calendars, societies and landscapes extended to myth and music. Traditional tales of the countryside were woven into a 12-part mythic cycle, exemplified by the 12 exploits of Gilgamesh, the 12 Labours of Hercules, the 12 stages in the story of Samson and the 12 adventuring knights

Fig. 1a. An astrological order was originally behind the pantheon of 12 Roman gods, here displayed on an ancient altar.

Fig. 1b. The 12 Greek gods and goddesses, each with a characteristic emblem, corresponded to the 12 zodiacal signs.

of King Arthur. Each of the episodes in these sagas was located in one of the 12 tribal divisions of the country. Similarly with music, the native songs were encoded within a 12-part chant, reproducing the music of the heavenly spheres, and each part of the chant was attached to one of the 12 tribes and their particular region. Thus in every possible way, from their astrological social order to their maintenance of a perpetual cycle of myth and music throughout the year, the inhabitants of a country were placed in harmony with the celestial realm and the rhythms of nature.

In the legends of quests for the Grail or some other talisman of divine rule, and in the histories of esoteric revivalist movements, there are commonly 12 participants, with or without a central thirteenth. The followers of Odysseus, like those of King Arthur, were 12 in number, and Charlemagne's mystical court consisted

Fig. 2. The six original tribes of Tibet are symbolized by the six red rays on the Tibetan national flag. In some accounts there are said to have been twelve Tibetan tribes whose representatives formed the circular council under the Dalai Lama.

of 12 peers who reclined on 12 beds around his magnificent couch. The same ritual order was adopted by the legendary rulers of old Ireland, as in the royal hall of King Conchobar of Ulster whose central couch was surrounded by those of his 12 principal warriors. A Pictish alliance, the 12 kings of Orkney under King Lot, is mentioned in Malory's *Morte d'Arthur*. King Hrolf of Denmark and his 12 berserkers are one of many such groups in Scandinavian legend. According to René Guénon there are 12 Rosicrucian adepts, and another 12 make up the inner circle of Agartha, the enchanted country now lost to sight, which was once paradise on earth.

The Knights Templar, founded in the twelfth century to safeguard Christian pilgrims to the Holy Land, followed in their constitution the traditional 12-fold pattern. A college of 12 electors, together with a chaplain, chose their grand master, who was attended by 12 servants, each with a separate, astrologically related function. An élite band of 12 Templars, consisting of ten knights and two commanders, were charged with protecting the relics of the True Cross in the Church of the Holy Sepulchre at Jerusalem. This symbolism was ostensibly derived from Jesus and the 12 disciples, and the chaplain who made the thirteenth member of the electoral college was said to represent the spirit of Christ. Yet the Templars' mystical rites were from an older tradition than Christianity. They were accused of celebrating the pagan mysteries in which candidates for initiation were subjected to 12 trials, three by each of the four elements, and their 12-member groups, assembled round an enigmatic thirteenth figure, were compared to those of black magicians and witch covens.

Either through esoteric tradition or spontaneously, significant groups of 12 recur in all ages. Many countries attribute their Christian conversion to a party of 12 missionaries, sometimes with a thirteenth as leader. St Joseph of Arimathaea, who brought Christianity and the Grail vessel to England soon after the Crucifixion, was one of 12 hermits, as were St Shio who converted Georgia and Alskik who turned the Icelanders to Christianity in the tenth century. St Petroc of Cornwall, St Ilid of Wales and St Columban of Gaul are among many founding saints who were attended by 12 companions.

Administrators also favour the number 12. King Charles, the great fourteenth-century ruler of Bohemia, built two great roads crossing at Prague to divide his country into four quarters, and subdivided it into 12 provinces; the Norman conquerors of southern Italy administered it as 12 provinces, each ruled by a count; Napoleon had 12 marshals; in wartime Germany Himmler furnished a Grail castle at Wewelsburg as a place of meeting and ritual for his inner council of 12 SS officers. A more appealing institution was the Royal College of Constantinople in the tenth century, where the president was styled the Sun of Science and his 12 associates, professors of the various arts and faculties, were each identified with one of the signs of the zodiac. Their library consisted of 36,500 volumes, a book for every day in a century.

This catalogue of twelves is greatly expanded in the following pages, but the above sample is enough to indicate how deep rooted is the practice of recognizing 12 zodiacal and psychological types and constructing calendars, theologies and societies on a duodecimal foundation. The tradition has been known in almost the same form from the Pacific islands to northern Scandinavia. Nor is it confined to the continents of Asia and Europe. The twelve-fold pattern is also found in Africa, in Egypt and the north, among the tribes of the west coast and in the island of Madagascar to the south-east. In America it was established long before the European invasions. The Aztec zodiac had 12 signs similar to those of the Chinese. The Mayans told of 12 paths by which their tribes had miraculously crossed the ocean to inhabit Yucutan, and 12 priests presided over their religious initiations. In North America the Pueblo Indians also recognized 12 religious orders. South of the Great Lakes, the Winnebago Indians had a 12-clan society, in which four superior clans represented the heavenly quarters.

Many other nations were arranged in a four-fold cosmological order of four cardinal points with a central fifth, and in some cases a 12-tribe subdivision is implied. The land of the Incas was divided in this way into four sectors, north, south, east and west, and was known as the Four Quarters of the World. In its capital, Cuzco, a sacred king, who was regarded as a descendant of the sun, was the centre of a constant ritual, and a national council was attended by the kings of the four districts and lesser tribal rulers. Examples of this pattern begin with the five sacred mountains of China, and of other eastern countries, four at each of the quarters and one at the centre. The natural, geometric development of a ring of 12 evenly spaced points from the basic 5-mountain plan is shown in *3a-d* figures 3a-c, alongside another interesting 12-part division of the circle (3d).

The supremacy of 12 among symbolic numbers is challenged only by the number 7. In every living organism these numbers are symbolically reconciled, for as 12 is the number of form and structure, 7 is the number of spirit. Thus we hear of 7 mountains in a sacred landscape, 7 colours in the rainbow, the 7 metals of alchemy, 7 *chakras* of the subtle body, 7 heavens, planes of consciousness, ages, archangels, candlesticks, pillars of wisdom, gifts of the spirit, virtues, vices, veils of mystery and many other 7-fold aspects of spiritual creation. At the head of all these are the 7 planets, the wandering lights that guided the migrations of the earliest tribes before the days of settlement and order, symbolized by the number 12. The planetary 7 are the archaic deities, preceding the zodiacal 12, and by 7 we naturally orientate ourselves within our three-dimensional universe; for there are 7 types of motion: left, right, forward, back, up, down and revolving in the centre. These 7 motions were associated by the Pueblo Indians of New Mexico with their 7 tribes, 7 cities and the 7-part division of their villages. The two-dimensional plan of these motions shows only five points (the up-and-down motions coinciding with the central point) and thus reproduces the plan of the 5 sacred mountains; from which we see that the sacred five are also the seven, corresponding to the 7 planets and the notes of the 7-holed flute which ruled the human soul in times before civilization.

The pattern we are here chiefly investigating is the 12-sided foundation plan of civilized order, which philosophers have acclaimed as providing the best possible world-view for societies

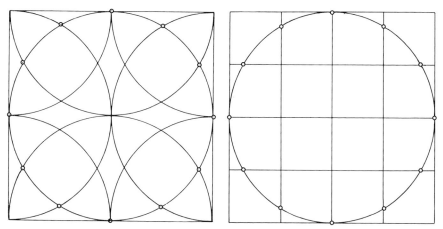

Figs. 3a and b. Two methods by which a geometer can divide the rim of a circle into 12 equal parts are shown above. In the second example, the containing square is divided into 16 smaller squares, and their points of intersection with the circle define the 12-part division. Below (*figs. 3c and d*) are two of the many possible designs developed from these constructions.

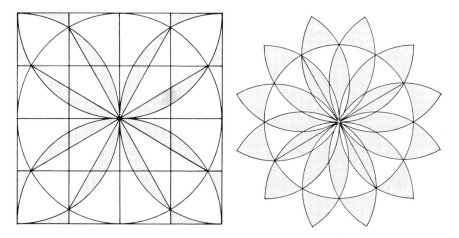

and individuals alike. The basis of that claim is that it is all-inclusive, enfolding the 7 hills and springs, the 5 mountains and 4 quarters in perfect harmony within the embrace of the zodiacal twelve. The more deeply we study the universal tradition of 12-tribe societies, the more splendidly apparent becomes the idea behind it: to create and maintain a perfectly balanced human order in harmony with the heavenly order, where life is experienced on a high level of spiritual intensity, as traditionally follows from the discovery of the Grail.

2

The classical amphictyonies

THE TWELVE-TRIBE AMPHICTYONIES OF
GREECE AND ASIA MINOR

Strabo in his *Geography* tells the story of how the ancient Athenians were divided into 12 parts by their ruler, Cecrops. The 12 districts they occupied were called Cecropia, Tetrapolis, Epacoia, Deceleia, Eleusis, Aphidua, Thoricus, Branron, Cytherus, Sphettus, Cephisia. The text here is corrupt and in some manuscripts only eleven names are given, but others add a twelfth, Phalerus. Theseus is said to have formed the 12 into one city, that of today. In earlier times the Athenians were ruled by kings, but later they fell into democracy.

In the *Athenian Constitution* Aristotle gives further details. First, he says, the Athenians were separated into quarters by King Panion, whose four sons were made rulers of the four parts. Theseus completed the 12-tribe pattern and related it to the calendar.

They were made into four groups in imitation of the seasons of the year. Each group was split into three tribes, making 12 in all, the same number as the months... The tribes each consisted of 30 clans, like the days in a month, and there were 30 men to each clan.

The most significant of the symbolic numbers in this scheme is not openly mentioned; such is the habit of esoteric philosophers. One is meant to calculate for oneself that the total number of Athenians was 10,800. That number indicates that Athens was placed under the goddess, the lunar deity, for, in the language of number symbolism, 1080 means the spirit of the earth and the mystical or feminine side of nature, influenced by the moon whose actual radius is 1080 miles. An image invoked by these associations is the wise, nocturnal owl, emblem of ancient Athens and Athena's companion.

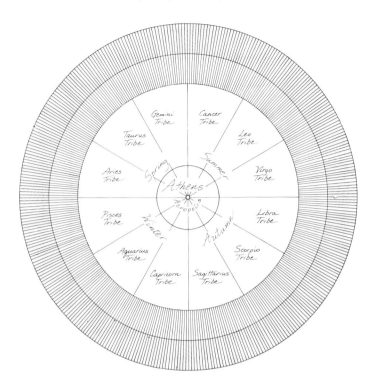

Fig. 4. The symbolic constitution of Athens as described by Aristotle. The 30 clans to each of the 12 tribes are represented by the 360 outer divisions which correspond to the 360 degrees of a circle.

The schematic diagram of Athens has the sanctuary on the Acropolis, with the axis of the universe imagined as passing through it, at the centre of the city. The four quarters and the twelve tribes are defined by radii, and the 360 families become the 360 degrees of the zodiacal or any other circle. There are thirty men in each family or clan, and if they are all allowed wives, they represent the sixty minutes in every degree. In that case their total number is twice 10,800 or 21,600, the number of minutes in a circle, as well as ten times the 2160 years in one astrological month, during which the sun runs its course through one of the signs of the zodiac.

This scheme of numerical and astronomical symbolism, varying only in detail, was adopted by nations throughout the Mediterranean lands, the Middle East and far beyond, but the most numerous examples, recorded by early historians, are found in

Greece. The tradition of 12-tribe unions was known to all the Greek peoples, the Ionians, the Dorians and the Aeolians. Such associations were called amphictyonies, meaning dwellers round a central shrine.

The most famous of Greek amphictyonies was centred on Mount Parnassus and the temple of Apollo at Delphi. According to Fabre d'Olivet it was founded by Orpheus, and the 12 tribes that formed it were said originally to have been a choral union. The names of the tribes were: the Thessalians, Boeotians, Dorians, Ionians, Perrhaebians, Magnetes, Locrians, Oetaens, Phthiotes, Malians, Phocians and Dolopians. Their territories met about twenty miles north of Delphi, near Thermopylae, where the temple of Demeter at Anthela was their other, and probably their earliest, sanctuary. The sacred mountain above it is Oeta, where once blazed the funeral pyre of Hercules.

Spring and autumn meetings of the amphictyonic council, the Pylaea, were held both at Delphi and Thermopylae. Every tribe sent a delegation of six men, consisting of two full councillors each with two juniors. With the rise of Delphi to become the most popular centre of pilgrimage in Greece, the duties of the Pylaea increased in scale and importance. It administered the shrine, organized its games and festivals, managed its estates and finances, maintained its temples, defended its rights and protected pilgrims. The 12 tribes were each and all responsible for looking after the sacred roads to Delphi which passed through their territory. Their most troublesome task was preventing or punishing trespasses on the lands sacred to Apollo, which extended over a large area. On several occasions, notably in the fourth century BC, they had recourse to warfare against sacrilegious offenders.

The Pylaea of the Delphic amphictyony was for centuries the supreme religious authority in Greece. Its influence faded under the dominance of Rome, but it was recorded as still existing in the second century BC.

The small but pre-eminently sacred island of Delos is marked by its legends as an archaic omphalos and the hub of a zodiacal circle. It is the smallest of the Cycladean group, a granite sliver 3 miles long from north to south and less than a mile wide, but it was said to be the parent of the other islands, which arranged themselves round it in a ring. Their collective name implies a circle, and on Delos the sacred lake was called, according to

Herodotus, the Wheel. Both Apollo and Artemis were born beside the Wheel, and to them the island was dedicated. The temples to various gods in its sacred precinct were dominated by the great Apollo temple with a colossal statue of the god beside it. Above it, on the summit of Mount Cynthus, was another temple, and on Cynthus is the oldest of the island's shrines, a sacred cavern.

From before the seventh century BC, Delos was the centre of an amphictyony, and Apollo's shrine was the focus of a great spring festival of music, games and ceremonies. Little is known about the Delian amphictyony, but in form, as in function, it probably reflected the 12-tribe organization of Delphi. Such was its prestige that, after the Persian war, when the Aegean cities formed a political alliance, they fixed their headquarters on Delos and made the temple of Apollo the ritual centre of their league. The organization became dominated by the Athenians, who removed its treasury and political institutions to their city, and the importance of Delos diminished. Yet the island retained its special sanctity throughout pagan times. The Athenians in 426 BC expressed their veneration by ritually purifying it, removing all tombs and even for a time expelling its native population. No one who appeared likely to die or give birth was allowed on the island.

Delphi, Athens, Delos; we observe that these three sanctuaries, the greatest religious centres in ancient Greece, stand together on one straight line. The writer who first pointed this out, Jean Richer, identifies this line as the major axis of Greek sacred geography, the symbolic pole of the universe for the entire Attic world. We write about Richer's further discoveries in chapter 8, and in chapter 9 we tell the remarkable story of what was disclosed when the Richer axis was extended into north-west Europe.

About 45 miles west of Delphi, the amphictyony of the warlike Aetolian tribes was located at Thermon, where their temple of Apollo was built in the seventh century BC. It occupied a magnificent site, high up on cliffs above Lake Tritonis but sheltered by surrounding peaks, a place of warm springs with an impressive air of sanctity.

To the south, across the Gulf of Corinth, is Achaea, where 12 small but independent towns formed an ancient amphictyony. Herodotus gives their names as: Pallene, Aegira, Aegae, Bura, Helice, Aegium, Rhypes, Patres, Phares, Olenus, Dyme and Tritaees. Their common meeting-place and ritual centre was the temple of Poseidon at Helice, which was overwhelmed by a sea flood in the fourth century BC. Assemblies were then held at the temple of Zeus in Aegium, and later they took place annually at each of the 12 towns in turn. The Achaean federal institution conducted warfare and diplomacy; otherwise the individual towns retained complete autonomy.

The Ionian league was a dodecapolis, an alliance of 12 cities in Asia Minor on the east coast of the Aegean. Its members were Miletus, Myrus, Priene, Ephesus, Colophon, Lebedus, Teos, Clazomenae, Phocaea, Erythraea and the islands of Samos and Chios. Originally they were ruled by kings with the King of Ephesus as chief. Their national sanctuary was the temple of Poseidon on the north slope of Mount Mycale, a promontory overlooking the sea. The assembly there was called the Pan-Ionion. Herodotus says that the Ionian dodecapolis was a continuation of a previous system in their former territories on the Peloponnese, whence they were expelled by the Achaeans.

To the north of the Ionians lived the Aeolians who also formed a 12-city organization, made up of Cyme, Larissa, Neon Tichus, Temnus, Cilla, Notium, Aegiroessa, Pitane, Aegaeae, Myrina, Grynea and Smyrna. They were reduced to eleven when Smyrna was taken from them by the Ionians, its citizens being distributed among the remaining cities. The great sacred mountain in their country was Mount Sipylos, where the gigantic effigy of a Hittite goddess is carved high up on the rock.

5   In addition to these, a number of other leagues or amphictyonies are mentioned by old historians. There are references to amphictyonies in Arcadia, at Onchestus beside Lake Copais and at Corinth beneath the sacred Acro-Corinth mountain. Leagues or federations of city-states are recorded in Lycia, Phocis, Akarnania, Epiros, Boeotia and elsewhere. A legend of Troy is that it was head of a 12-city league in the time of King Priam. Not all federations were of strictly 12 members. The Dorians had a hexapolis, and later there arose groups of 5, 7, 30 and other numbers. Twelve, however, was the original and conventional number in such unions.

Their archaic foundation myths, and their beginnings as 12 tribes rather than cities, indicate the antiquity of Greek amphicytonies. At some early period tribes of the same culture and language, throughout Greece and beyond, formed themselves into 12 units according to a standard cosmological pattern. Their meetings were

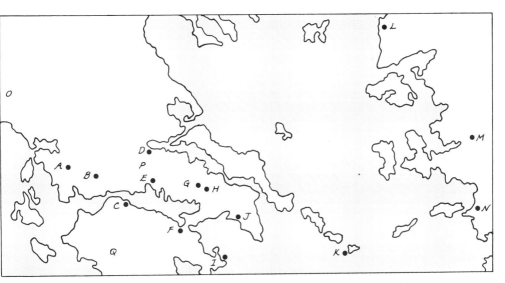

Fig. 5. Sites of known amphictyonies and leagues in the ancient Greek world.

A Stratos (centre of Akarnanian league).
B Thermon (Aetolian league).
C Aegium (later centre of Achaean league).
D Thermopylae (Delphic amphictyony).
E Delphi (Delphic amphictyony).
F Corinth (Corinthian amphictyony).
G Onchestus (amphictyony of Onchestus).
H Thebes (Boeotian league).
I Kalauria (Kalaurian amphictyony).

J Athens (Athenian amphictyony).
K Delos (Delian amphictyony).
L Troy (Trojan amphictyony).
M Mount Sipylos (Aeolian amphictyony).
N Mount Mycale (Ionian league).
O Epiros (Epirote league, centre unidentified).
P Phocis (Phocian league, centre unidentified).
Q Arcadia (Arcadian league, centre. unidentified).

held on or below a sacred mountain, and the country around it belonged to no one tribe but was shaped as an image of paradise and dedicated to the 12 gods.

Ever since people began to live in cities, the problem has been to preserve the harmony and sacred values of primordial life while enjoying the comforts of civilization. The attempted solution was to preserve the forms of the ancient 12-tribe system by the astrological apportionment of settled landscapes between 12 cities. Local mythologies told how these allotments were first ruled by gods and then by mortal kings who maintained the divine ritual and code of knowledge. According to Strabo, the 12 parts of Achaea were previously governed by kings, as was the case in Ionia. When the tribal people settled in towns and villages, their mutual business was conducted by deputies, usually from the aristocracy. The growth of commerce and imperialism converted the old amphictyonies into political and military alliances. Their sacred functions declined, traditions were forgotten and they fell prey in the end to the dissolving influence of democracy or tyranny.

Yet the traditional pattern of twelve around a central thirteenth has never entirely been forgotten. The Greeks of historical times made many attempts to renew the old enchantment by constructing 12-city constitutions, and Plato in the fourth century BC, when the sacred 12-tribe structures had given way to political and commercial unions, drew up a ground plan in the *Laws* for its revival. As an archetypal pattern it haunts the imagination, occurs spontaneously to the idealistic mind and is always a potential source of inspiration and renaissance.

THE TWELVE CITIES OF ETRURIA

Dodecapolis organizations, essentially the same as those of Greece and elsewhere, existed in Italy from ancient times and are recorded by Roman and Greek historians. Best known is the 12-city league of the Etruscan heartland, now Tuscany, and two or three other such Etruscan groups are mentioned. Neighbouring people, the Samians, Hernicans and the Volscians, also had sacred unions of cities.

6 The names of the venerable Etruscan twelve cities are not completely known, neither has the exact site of their central shrine and meeting-place ever been discovered. It was the Fanum or sacred place of Voltumna who was originally an underworld goddess, assuming fantastic shapes and ruling over the world of vegetation. She was later seen as an hermaphrodite, Voltumnus-

7 Voltumna, and was known to the Romans as Vertumnus. Her temple is believed to have been in the region of Volsini to the east of Lake Bolsena. Scholars have generally located it on the southeast shore of the lake near Montefiascone, and Jean Richer plausibly suggests that it was on the present site of the church of San Flaviano in the centre of the town, where an ancient platform may have been the footing of the Etruscan temple.

Every year the Etruscans gathered at the Fanum Voltumnae for a national festival and trading fair, where 'solemn games' were held, a religious synod debated matters of ritual and representatives

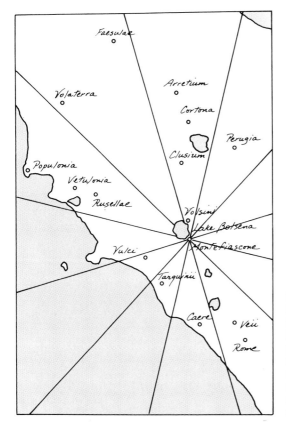

Fig. 6. The cities of ancient Etruria to the north of Rome included the 12 members of the Etruscan league. Their positions are shown here, together with a suggested scheme of the symbolic division of the country into 12 sectors from the ritual centre near Lake Bolsena.

of the twelve cities took council together. In early days the delegates were kings of their respective tribes, and one of their number presided as high king. By the fourth century the kings had been replaced by 12 aristocratic officials. Their emblem of office was the 12 *fasces*, a bundle of rods and an axe, which, in times of war, were given to a supreme commander. When the Etruscans finally surrendered to Rome, they submitted the 12 *fasces*, which were afterwards carried by the Roman magistrates. The Romans were proud of Etruscan antiquity; it became fashionable among them to claim Etruscan lineage and to attend the traditional games at the Fanum Voltumnae.

Speculation about the origin of the Etruscan twelve cities was current even in Roman times. Most of the old historians theorized that the Etruscans had originated in the eastern Mediterranean area, but Dionysius, who made a special study of the subject,

Fig. 7. Vertumnus, the male aspect of the archaic Etruscan deity of vegetation and fertility, is here depicted by the fantastical sixteenth-century artist Arcimboldo. The composition of fruits and vegetables also served as a portrait of the Emperor Rudolf II.

concluded that they were indigenous to Italy. The fact that their 12-city system so exactly paralleled those of ancient Greece does not mean that it originated there, for such systems have been found among native people worldwide. The history of the Etruscan organization followed a common pattern. Beginning as an amphictyony, a sacred commonwealth of 12 tribes and 12 kings in the canonical mode, it developed into a league of 12 cities who were forced into temporary political union by the pressure of warfare.

Livy and other historians tell of a dodecapolis in northern Italy, above the river Po. Its legendary foundation was by 12 groups of colonists from Etruria. Neither its constitution nor the names of its component cities are known, but its centre may have been at Mantua, for Virgil described that city as being 'rich in ancestry, but of different races. There are three races there, each divided into four peoples.'

Also said to be of Etruscan origin was a dodecapolis in Campania, to the south of Rome. Its chief city was Capua, and among the twelve were probably Nola, Pompeii, Herculaneum and Sorrento. Again there is no full list of the cities nor any records of how they conducted their affairs.

THE TWELVE GALLIC TRIBES

At the time of Caesar's conquest, the four main tribes of Gaul, the Carnutes, the Bituriges, the Arvernes and the Eduens, occupied territories around the geographical and ritual centre of the country. This was the site of the present town of Châteaumeillant, formerly Mediolanum, a name which has the same meaning as Milan, the Middle Land. Other such names are Myon in France, Meon in Britain (and possibly Meriden in Warwickshire, the traditional centre of England) and Midhe, the middle province of Ireland. Mediolanum was in the territory of the Bituriges, and nearby in the land of the Carnutes was the ritual and legislative centre for the federation of Gaulish tribes where, according to Caesar, their Grand Council was held.

According to Geoffrey of Monmouth's *History of the Kings of Britain*, ancient Gaul was ruled by 12 kings of equal rank. Uniting their 12 armies, they made common cause against Brutus and his Trojan warriors who were passing through Gaul on their way to Britain. A more historical record of a Gaulish 12-tribe federation occurs in Strabo's *Geography*. It concerns the tribes of Galatia. They were a Gaulish people who migrated from their homeland in the third century BC and took possession of the central highland region of Asia Minor. At first they travelled as three tribes but, when they settled, each tribe was divided into four 'tetrarchies', thus creating the traditional 12-fold order. Each of the 12 sections was governed by a chief and a judge who was probably of the Druidic order. The other officials were a military commander and two subordinates. The tetrarchies administered their own affairs, but for mutual business and to judge serious crimes such as murder they each sent twenty-five representatives to a national council of three hundred. These meetings were held at the central Galatian sanctuary, a place called Drunemeton. Nemeton means the same as Mediolanum, the navel of the earth, and the prefix Dru is taken as a reference to their Druid priesthood.

3

Scandinavia

THE TWELVE GODS OF ODIN

Odin, the divine ancestor of the Norsemen, inhabited a region called Midgard, the middle space or world centre. It was surrounded by a circular wall and rings of mountains and oceans, and within 8 it lay Asgard, home of the Asar, the 12 gods. Odin sat amid them on his high throne. They were attended by an equivalent number of goddesses headed by Frigg, Odin's consort. In Asgard they feasted and gave laws and judgments, setting an example for the human race which enjoyed a golden age under their guidance.

Under Christianity the gods were demoted to legendary heroes. The thirteenth-century Icelandic historian, Snorri Sturluson, traced their genealogy from Zeus through King Priam of Troy, who ruled over a league of 12 cities. Priam's grandson was Thor, and of the same line twenty generations later was born Odin. He was the king of Asaland in Asia, east of the river Don. In his capital, Asgard, was the national temple where 12 lordly priests made sacrifices and upheld the laws. Asaland was divided into 12 parts by 12 rivers which flowed from the horns of a stag beneath the tree at the centre of the world. Their names form an incantation and, if read aloud, produce the sound of water bubbling from a spring or bottle:

Sid, Vid, Sekin, Ekin, Svöl, Gunnthro, Fjörm, Fimbulthul, Gipul, Göpul, Gömul, Geirvimul.

Threatened by invasion from Rome, Odin left his homeland and led a migration northwards. With many followers he passed through Germany, France and Scandinavia and established a new Asgard in Sweden. Thus the origins of Scandinavian culture derived from the Greek gods and the 12 cities of Troy.

In all countries where Odin and the 12 gods were worshipped, ritual centres, or Things, were designed on the pattern of Asgard. Such places were at Tingwall in the Shetland Islands, Dingwall in

Fig. 8. Valhalla, Odin's dwelling with twelve doors,
as depicted in the seventeenth-century Copenhagen manuscript.

Scotland and the Tynwald on the Isle of Man, where the island's laws are still proclaimed from an artificial mound, traditionally composed of earth from twelve parts of the country. National Things were held at Jelling in Denmark and Uppsala in Sweden. In Norway the division of the whole country into four quarters was instituted as a revival of ancient usage by King Haakon the Good in the tenth century AD. The quarters were each divided into three Thing districts, which settled their own affairs subject to the greater authority of the central Thing of their quarter.

The 12 gods ruled over the 12 Thing districts, and their place of assembly, Odin's palace in Asgard, was represented by the

Althing, the national council, which was attended by 12 priestly deputies from each of the four quarters. Two advisers were allowed to every deputy, bringing the total number of those seated at the Althing to 144. They took their places on three benches, forty-eight to a bench, around the Thing floor. With them was an elaborate array of lesser officials, hereditary, nominated or elected, and beyond the inner ring was the assembly of people. Thus the administration of law and justice was performed in the manner of sacred theatre, on a mythological level, as if the gods were still ruling on earth.

Twelve was the customary number of magistrates who sat together at Scandinavian Things, and the same number today makes up an Anglo-Saxon jury. Another group who followed the gods of Odin in forming bands of twelve were the berserkers. These élite warriors, who seem from their legends to have been a mixture between Arthurian knights and Hell's Angels, were initiated into the sacred mysteries of their profession and each had an affinity with a certain beast whose spirit they would invoke in battle. Thus they gained a reputation for shape-shifting, taking on the forms of bears or wolves. They fought without armour in a state of induced frenzy which made them impervious to fear or wounds. Many of the legendary and early Norse kings retained bands of 12 berserkers as well as bodyguards of 12 or more disciplined warriors, their champions.

THE ZODIACAL WHEEL OF ASGARD

9   The names of the twelve followers of Odin, as given by Snorri Sturluson, are: Thor, Njörd, Freyr, Tyr, Heimdall, Bragi, Ull, Hoenir, Forseti, Loki, Balder, Hoder.

Each of these represents an aspect of Odin. He corresponds to the Roman god Mercury, who also had twelve other names, and he is commemorated through the Anglo-Saxon version of his name, Woden, in Wednesday or Woden's day. Wednesday is the middle day of the week, and Odin's place within the zodiac wheel of Asgard is also central. His followers, drawn up in a circle around him, correspond to the 12 astrological signs. There is no authoritative guide to their proper order or to the signs which they each represent, but the clues provided by their various legends suggest the following arrangement.

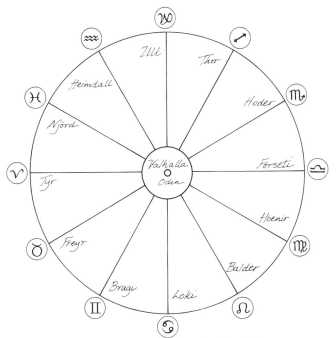

Fig. 9. Zodiac of the gods of Valhalla.

Aries is Tyr whose name is the origin of Tuesday. He was a brave warrior and gave victory in battle. He lost a hand in his encounter with the monster Fenrir.

Taurus is Freyr who was mild, joyful and lovely. She gave sunshine and rain, peace and abundance.

Gemini is Bragi who was brilliant, eloquent and poetic.

Cancer is Loki, the trickster and mercurial shape-shifter. He gave birth to the world serpent and to Hel, ruler of the underworld. He is similar to Hermes whom Athanasius Kircher equates with Cancer.

Leo is Balder, fair-haired and white of skin, radiant and beautiful, wise and merciful. All the trees and metals swore they would never hurt him. Only the mistletoe was not bound by this oath, and Hoder the blind god was tricked by Loki into killing Balder with a mistletoe spear.

Virgo is Hoenir, keen of mind and perception, whose silence was a sign of his prophetic wisdom. He was present at the birth of the human race on whom he bestowed intelligence. Sometimes

10

31

called Longfoot, he was the companion of Odin and Loki in their wanderings.

Libra is Forseti who dispensed justice in a hall made equally of gold and silver. His cult is said to have spread northwards from Frisia, where a saga credits him with the introduction of law. It says that Charles the Great demanded of 12 Frisian elders that they should recite him their laws, and when they could not obey he set them adrift at sea in a rudderless boat. In their predicament they called for divine help, and were answered by the appearance of a stranger in their boat. He bore a golden axe, and with it he steered the boat towards land. As they approached the shore he flung out his axe, and where it fell to ground a spring welled up. The stranger, who was Forseti in disguise, taught the Frisians a code of law and then vanished.

Scorpio is Hoder, the blind god of darkness and war. In the story of how he was tricked by Loki into killing Balder (Leo) with the mistletoe spear can be seen the god of winter piercing the fullness of summer at the autumnal equinox.

Sagittarius is Thor, remembered in the name of Thursday. He was born out of earth by Odin and took precedence after Odin above the other gods. As god of thunder, he was armed with the magical hammer Mjöllnir.

Capricorn is Ull, famed for his skills in archery and skiing. One of his emblems was a shield which sometimes served him as a boat.

Aquarius is Heimdall, guardian of the gods and keeper of the rainbow bridge between heaven and earth. Through his wonderful horn he could hear everything, even the wool growing on a sheep's back. He dwelt in the mountain at the centre of the world. The Ugro-Finnish tribes represented him by a standing pillar, as Apollo and Hermes were represented in Greece, and his attributes resemble those of St Michael.

Pisces is Njörd who controlled the winds and oceans and gave health and riches. A northern aquatic plant is called Njörd's glove.

THE ENCHANTMENT OF ICELAND

From Norway and other northern countries, between 870 and 930 AD, came the pioneer settlers of Iceland. They brought furnishings and sacred earth from their homeland temples, and discovered by

Fig. 10. The topographical symbols of Odin's realm are combined in this
image of the world centre in relation to lower planes of existence.

divination favourable sites in the new country for their first farms
and sanctuaries. Their only recorded predecessors in Iceland were
some Irish monks who, it is said, left as the new settlers arrived.

An intriguing mystery surrounds the early days of the colony.
Its leaders were mainly worshippers of Odin and the 12 Norse
gods, but among them were Celtic Christians from Ireland, the
Hebrides and the Isle of Man. From the very start they followed
an agreed pattern of settlement, acceptable to both pagans and
Christians because it belonged exclusively to no one religion but
reflected a universal tradition.

The whole island was divided into four quarters: north, south, 11
east and west. They administered their affairs independently but
according to the same method. Each quarter was subdivided into
three sections, with a chief elected governor and two subordinates
to rule the sections on either side of him. Thus there were 12
sections in Iceland and 12 legislative Things, four of them being

33

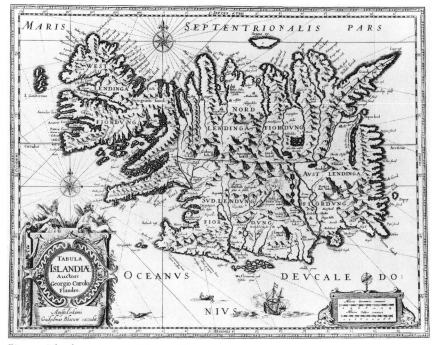

Fig. 11. The four ritual divisions of Iceland: north, south, east and west.

dominant. Likewise there were four paramount and eight lesser governors, each with two subordinates, making thirty-six *godi* or priest-chieftains in all. They presided over their local Things, and at midsummer they met at the Althing, the national assembly, established in 930 at Thingvellir in the south-western part of the island, thirty miles from Reykjavik.

The president of the Althing was a learned scholar, the law-speaker, who was elected for a period of three years. During his time in office he had to recite from memory the entire body of Icelandic law in verse form to the *godi* and the people, who assembled in great numbers on the plain below the Law Rock on which he stood. They came from all over the country, trekking on ponies for many days across the pathless wastes, guided on their way by stone cairns erected on high places. A tented camp was set up on the plain of Thingvellir, and a three-week festival was held with games, athletic contests, music and bardic competitions.

Fig. 12. W. G. Collingwood's nineteenth-century depiction of Iceland's traditional midsummer gathering, the Althing. It was held below a towering rock where the island's main geological fault had caused a dramatic rift.

Trade and business were conducted and marriages arranged. Meanwhile, at the formal assembly, laws and treaties were enacted, and a bench of thirty-six judges held court. Every free man in Iceland had access to the Althing.

The central regions of Iceland are mostly frozen desert, so the Althing, though conceptually in the middle of the country, was not geographically so. It took a year's search before its correct site was located, and the spot was obviously chosen for its outstanding magical qualities. It is a narrow chasm where two walls of rock have been split apart along Iceland's main geological fault line. A rock beside its deepest fissure became the lawspeaker's rostrum. In all old religions such places are sacred to the powers of the earth which are concentrated there. As a magical centre and place of 12-tribe assembly, Thingvellir is comparable to Delphi.

This magical constitution immediately gave rise to a remarkably rich culture, which each of the four quarters developed in distinctive

12

35

forms. Its most famous product is the Icelandic sagas. These recitations of heroic exploits are closely linked to the features of the landscapes in which they are set, and thus reflect the characters of their respective regions. From the sagas and the early Icelandic histories much is to be learnt about the original sacred foundation pattern and the natural landmarks to which it was tied. The overall picture is of a whole country placed under a carefully woven spell. Herein lies the problem which perplexes modern academic students of ancient Iceland and of other states organized on the traditional pattern. Behind their economic and social structures, which can be studied by modern methods, there is evidently a further dimension which eludes materialistic analysis because it has to do with the spirit. The founders of Iceland possessed the traditional science of making a country habitable, not merely on a level of economic subsistence, but spiritually also, allowing the simple homestead-dwellers to experience lives of rich, full quality, as if in a golden age of mythology or under the enchantment of the Grail.

Over the last forty years an Icelandic scholar, Einar Palsson, has studied the native sagas, histories, traditions, antiquities and landscapes in quest of the science which produced such an immediately rich culture – not only in Iceland but in all countries where its relics have been discerned. His eight-volume work, *The Roots of Icelandic Culture*, is published in Icelandic only, but some of his papers have been translated into English, and these make a valuable contribution to studies of the ancient tradition.

In many countries the rulers of 12 tribes and land divisions were under the ritual leadership of a central thirteenth, a sacred king. He was symbolically wedded to the nature goddess of the country, and at his coronation was charged with the magical power which gave him influence over the weather, the health and fertility of his realm and the order of nature generally. He was like the sun around which the planets revolve and the supreme god at the centre of the zodiacal twelve. In pagan Iceland there was no such figure, but Palsson suggests that there was nevertheless a sacred monarchy, kingship being exercised collectively by the thirty-six priest-chieftains who met at the Althing.

The crown, conceived of as a holy circle, was divided into its thirty-six components. Assembled at Thingvellir, the central Althing, the thirty-six formed one body politic, one kingship. Each of the thirty-six priest-chieftains was at the same time a secular and spiritual head of his domain... The priest-chieftains maintained the harmony of the interaction between man and the cosmos.

As in Britain where, in the days of the Celtic Church, Christian and pagan communities lived in mutual respect as neighbours, so it was in early Iceland. The Christians had a mystical leader, whom Palsson compares to the sacred king of Celtic lands. His spiritual powers augmented those of the thirty-six priest-chieftains, and he played a certain part in maintaining the enchanted realm. Palsson identifies him as the hereditary Keeper of the Grail.

Asolf Alskik, the first Christian missionary to arrive in Iceland, was accompanied by 12 followers. The country was officially converted in 1000 A D, but for long after that the influence of the priest-chieftains and their noble families remained in force. It was not until 1271, after the four quarters of Iceland had one by one lost their independence to the king of Norway, that their powers were finally broken by the imposition of an alien constitution. Also broken was the enchantment which produced and maintained a noble culture. The result was an immediate decline in all the arts of living. The skills which produced the great carved timber halls of the pagan chieftains were forgotten, and many of the crafts involved in fishing and agriculture fell into disuse. Farm carts and deep-sea vessels were no longer made. The vigorous culture of old Iceland gave way to apathy.

A renaissance began in the nineteenth century as native scholars rediscovered the greatness of their old culture. The Althing was reconstituted in 1874. With sixty elected deputies it now meets in Reykjavik. In 1944 Iceland gained full independence from Denmark, and thousands of people gathered at the old site at Thingvellir to hear the proclamation of the new Icelandic Republic.

4

Africa and Asia

EGYPT

According to the *History* of Herodotus, the Egyptians were the
first people to recognize a pantheon of 12 gods and to divide the
solar year into 12 months, each month being dedicated to one of
the gods. Later they divided all Egypt into 12 regions and appointed
a king over each. This commemorated a previous era when the
gods ruled in person over the 12 parts of the country. The 12 kings
were united by family ties and also by a strict treaty which they
renewed at regular formal meetings in one of the 12 temples.

Near the centre of their joint kingdom they constructed, by
diverting the waters of the Nile, a vast inland sea, the Lake of
Moeris, measuring some 3600 furlongs round its perimeter, about
the same length as the Egyptian coastline, with island pyramids in
the middle of it. Beside it they built the famous labyrinth, which
Herodotus called indescribably wonderful, estimating it as a greater
work than all the Greek temples and public buildings put together.
It stood between 12 covered courts, 6 on the north side and 6 on
the south, and consisted of 3000 apartments, half of them above
ground and half below. Herodotus was given a tour of the upper
chambers and galleries, but he was not allowed to see the lower
part which contained the tombs of kings and the sacred crocodiles.

The rule of 12 kings came to an end with the fulfilment of a
prophecy. An oracle had declared that whoever poured a libation
from a bronze cup in the temple of Hephaestus should become
king of all Egypt. The 12 kings were given gold cups when they
met at that temple, but on the final occasion the priests forgot to
give one of the kings his cup, and when his turn came, he poured
the libation from his bronze helmet. For this he was banished by
the others, but with the help of foreign mercenaries he attacked
and defeated the eleven kings and became sole monarch of Egypt.

The division of ancient Egypt into 12 separately administered nomes or provinces is mentioned by Strabo in the last of his seventeen volumes of *Geography*. Describing the labyrinth, he says that each of the nomes had a palace and courts therein, where they would assemble for religious festivals and to enact laws. Other writers record thirty-six nomes of Egypt, subdivisions of the original 12 corresponding to the thirty-six decans, three to each of the zodiacal signs.

WEST AFRICA

Traditions of 12-tribe leagues in Africa are mentioned by Dr Bähr in his two-volumed *Symbolik des mosaischen Kultus*. Best known is the confederation of 12 Ashanti tribes: the Bekwai, Adansi, Juabin, Kokofu, Kumasi, Mampon, Nsuta, Nkwanta, Dadiassi, Daniassi, Ofinsu and Adjisu. They were organized according to the conventional pattern, each tribe being ruled by its own king whose dynasty was of divine origin. The 12 kings, attended by courts of hereditary nobles, met in conclave each year. At the beginning of the eighteenth century the capital of the Ashanti tribes became fixed at Kumasi and the king of Kumasi presided over their meetings. The symbol of his high kingship was the golden stool on which he was crowned. The last king of the Ashanti nation was deposed and exiled by the British in 1896 and his territory was incorporated in the colony of the Gold Coast.

POLYNESIA AND THE BERBERS

Around the Hawaiian islands are said to be 12 other islands, now invisible, which form an earthly paradise inhabited by the gods. Their directions are known but one is not supposed to point towards them. The gods have hidden them and they are called the Lost Islands. The chants and myths in which they are described were known before the tenth century, when the Polynesians from Tahiti first settled in Hawaii. This implies that the 12 mythical islands were once more widely known across the Pacific. They may indeed be linked with the 12 recognized groups of Polynesian islanders, each speaking a dialect of their common language, whose

12 island territories (as named before modern political changes) are:

Hawaii, Ellice, Phoenix, Union, Manihiki, the Marquesas, Tonga, Samoa, Cook, Society, Tubuai and Tuamotu.

According to Max Freedom Long, the early expert on Polynesian magic and shamanism, there are in fact only eleven Polynesian tribes. In his book of 1948, *The Secret Science behind Miracles*, he tells the legend of the twelfth tribe, and how it became separated from the others.

Long's informant was a retired journalist, William Reginald Stewart, who had spent some time in North Africa being instructed by a native wise woman in the magical traditions of a certain Berber tribe. This tribe, he was told, was once one of twelve whose homeland was the Sahara, at a time when it was watered and fertile. With the onset of drought, the twelve tribes moved to the Nile valley and became masters of Egypt. They ruled by their magical arts which they also used to build the pyramids. There came a time when their prophets foresaw an age of darkness, when their ancient traditions would be threatened. To preserve their knowledge, they decided to disperse and to find refuge in the loneliest parts of the earth. Eleven of the tribes moved eastward, passing through the Red Sea and along the coasts of India or Africa towards the various groups of Pacific islands. The twelfth tribe went in the other direction, to the Atlas mountains.

This tribe spoke the Berber tongue of its neighbours, but also possessed a quite different, sacred language, reserved for magical purposes. Stewart learnt some of its phrases from his woman instructor, who was apparently the last of the tribal initiates. On reading Long's first book on the magic of the Polynesian *kahunas*, the native shamans, he was struck by the similarity between their religious terms and those of his Berbers. The word for a shaman, *kahuna*, was common to them both (though spelt *quahuna* by the Berbers); a female shaman, *kahuna wahini*, corresponded to the Africans' *quahuna quahini*; and *akua*, a god in Polynesian, was rendered *atua*. These and other parallels obviously indicated a single origin.

This account echoes Herodotus's story of the 12 kings and tribes of ancient Egypt, and Long also found it compatible with the migration legends of the Hawaiians. He was thus inclined to accept the testimony of Mr Stewart, and to derive the secret magical lore of the Polynesians, as well as of the Berbers, from Egypt and its legendary 12 tribes.

THE TWELVE KINGS OF MADAGASCAR

The huge island of Madagascar off the south-east coast of Africa *13* is almost 1000 miles long and its inhabitants are of various ethnic origins, Aboriginal, African, Malayan, Polynesian and others. Since 1960 they have been united in the Republic of Malagasy, but up to the time of the French invasion in 1896 they were in different tribes, though with a common language and similar forms of religion. During the nineteenth century the Hova of the central region, Imerina, became the dominant people. Their kings made treaties on behalf of the whole island with the United States and European powers, but this did not protect them from colonial aggression. Their capital, Antananarivo, was seized by a French

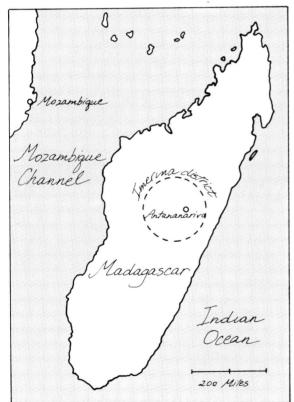

Fig. 13. The capital of Madagascar, Antananarivo, in the district of Imerina was the sacred city of the former 12-tribe Hova kingdom.

army, their last monarch, Queen Ranavalona III, was sent into exile, and the state system of Imerina was abolished.

The Hova administration of Imerina was a classic example of 12-tribe amphictyonic government. Antananarivo and the whole country around it were divided into four quarters, representing the four directions and seasons of the year, and a paramount chief was set over each division. The people were then subdivided into 12 tribes, each with its king and each corresponding to a zodiacal sign and month of the year. The 12 kings formed a state council to the high king at Antananarivo, whose attributes were those of a sacred ruler of divine descent. He was allowed 12 wives, one from each of the tribes. The 12 kings also claimed divine ancestors, gods who had previously ruled over the 12 parts of Imerina. Their shrines and idols stood in the 12 villages, each on a sacred hilltop which surrounded the capital, and there also were the tombs of their first royal descendants and their dynasties.

At important state festivals such as coronations, the 12 idols were brought together from the villages and made a procession through the capital, led by a thirteenth. Their astrological characters, and those of the tribes and regions they represented, were indicated by their names, which have been translated as: Small but Famous; Sole Sovereign; Able to Answer; He Who Can Conquer the Strong; He with Much Hair on the Back of his Neck; Great Hunter; He Who Strings Money (Enriches); Sleepless Creator; the Stake or Pin; the Crawling One; Red Coffer; Royal Prince.

The 12 royal families were an aristocratic, priestly class with a strict hierarchy of rank. They formed the court of the high king and provided his ministers. All royal proclamations were addressed to the twelve kings as guardians of the traditional order. There may also have been a similar, wider system to include all the Madagascan tribes, for the French administration recognized 12 different tribal provinces on the island.

After the fall of Antananarivo (now Gallicized as Tananarive), the new governor marked the end of the old enchantment by an appropriate symbolic act. On the spot where the 12 kings used to meet in council, he erected a bandstand, where the music of French military bands set the tone of the colonial regime.

The old traditions of Imerina were fast fading by the 1940s, when the anthropologist Mary Danielli made a study of what remained. She observed the close similarity between the state systems of Imerina and Iceland, and wondered how the same forms came to be repeated in such different places and ages. Evidently she was unaware how often and widely this same system has recurred, but she was shrewd in detecting a common underlying cosmology, which she compared to that of China. In Madagascar she studied the ways and traditions of the *mpanando*, the native diviners or geomancers, whose profession corresponds to that of the Chinese *feng shui* men. They take responsibility for the psychic wellbeing of families and regions, using their skill to determine the most propitious sites and designs for tombs, shrines, temples and domestic dwellings. Danielli found that the cosmological diagrams drawn up by the *mpanando* were the same as those in *feng shui* and were applied to the same purposes. On every scale, from the ritual division of the country to the arrangement of individual houses, the 12-fold astrological pattern was apparent. Thus the traditional Madagascan house is divided into 12 parts, each placed under one of 12 constellations, and daily activities therein are influenced by astrology.

There is much more we would like to know about Imerina's sacred geography and the ancient enchantments of Madagascar. Miss Danielli was not able to identify all the twelve former sacred villages; she believed that confusion had occurred at some time in the past, when the Hova capital was moved to Antananarivo from Ambohimanga, which is further south. No doubt the scholars of modern Madagascar have settled the problem and have reconstructed the old 12-tribe kingdom. The magic that sustained it is said still to be practised, despite the hostility of missionaries, by the native *mpanando*. We imagine this great, unreported island as a country still semi-enchanted, where among the strangest fauna and flora (including perhaps the rumoured man-eating tree) can be found some of the answers to the questions raised in this book.

THE TWELVE SAINTS OF GEORGIA

Georgia, now a republic in the Soviet Union, is the last Christian country of south-east Europe, and its history of repeated invasions by Turks, Persians, Asiatic tribes and other neighbours has made the Georgians vigorous in preserving their national traditions.

There are remarkable similarities between Georgian mythology and that of Scandinavia. In both is the image of the world-tree, linking heaven, earth and the underworld. To the Georgians it is an oak. From its summit there stretches upwards a gold chain, on which the gods descend to earth. A sacred oak was a feature of every old pagan sanctuary.

The memory of an ancient Georgian amphictyony survives in the folklore of Pshavi, a mountainous region to the north of the capital Tbilisi. There, it is said, is a spot where 12 tribes used to hold annual meetings. An oak with a golden chain marked the centre of their territory. The site, we are told, is known locally and is described in Georgian literature, but we have not been able to identify it.

More definite is the Georgian missionary legend, which attributes the implanting of Christianity there to a group of 12 holy anchorites in the fifth century. They were followers of Simeon Stylites, most of whose life was spent atop a pillar in the Syrian desert; thence they were called the Syrian Fathers. These 12 divided the new country up between them, each founding a community of hermits in some lonely spot. Their leader, St Shio, made his settlement at the end of a long valley by a spring surrounded by a horseshoe of steep cliffs. His disciples excavated cells in the cliff face, while the saint himself sought seclusion by the opposite method to St Simeon's, boring a shaft into the earth and spending his remaining years at the bottom of it. Over this sacred pit was later built the great monastery of Shio Mgvime.

The ascetic habits of the Syrian Fathers were much like those of their contemporaries, the Celtic saints, and their legends are also much the same. In extreme isolation they cultivated spiritual power, gaining control over wild animals, the forces of nature and their own minds and bodies. In the early days of Shio's settlement, provisions were carried up the valley by a feral wolf, spellbound by the saint's sanctity. Thus is symbolized the magical influence which the 12 Syrian fathers exerted over the tribes of Georgia.

The 12 missionaries to Georgia, the 12 under St Joseph who brought the Gospel to England, and the 12 followers of Asolf Alskik who converted Iceland conform to the same archetypal pattern. Behind that pattern we glimpse a traditional formula for bringing about that state which the Celts associate with the restoration of the Grail. Evidently it was known to the earliest Christians, who attempted in magical groups of 12 holy men to re-establish it in various countries.

CENTRAL ASIA AND THE MOUNTAIN AT
THE CENTRE OF THE WORLD

In legends and cosmologies throughout the whole of Asia are references to a central, pyramid-shaped mountain, which forms the polar axis of the world and provides the main link between heaven and earth. It is surrounded by a plain, which is the original Garden of Eden, and is divided into quarters by the four rivers of paradise. At the four quarters stand four lesser mountains, each with a distinctive shape as a symbol of one of the four elements. Further out are seven rings of mountains to represent the seven stages of creation, planetary orbits and many other things, and beyond are the four main island continents of the world, each flanked by two smaller islands. These 12 lands are sometimes depicted as 12 petals of a lotus.

14

This pattern occurs, in countless forms and variations, in temple paintings and mandorlas, in the plans, shapes and furnishings of temples, in the layout of cities and in the sacred geography of whole countries. Thus every state, and every region and settlement comprising it, was formed after the same model as an image of the original paradise. An example is China where four sacred mountains, with five-peaked, pyramidal Sung Shan as the central fifth, were seen as a large-scale version of the five-pillared Chinese temple. Similar world-views, in which the mother country at the centre was surrounded by four continents and 12 lands under 12 constellations, were officially upheld in Chaldaea from about 2000 BC, in Persia, India and every other centre of Eastern civilization. A Buddhist version is quoted by A. and B. Rees in *Celtic Heritage*.

The Kalmucks of Siberia picture the world as being circular with a square pyramidal mountain in the centre. In the ocean in each of the four directions is a separate quarter of the world. Each quarter consists of a large island with a small island on either side, making a total of twelve lands around a central mountain. The Kalmucks also associate a different colour with each direction, and with this may be compared the twelve winds of different colours described in a tenth-century Irish poem... Each of the four winds from the cardinal points is separated from the next by two subordinate winds.

In the course of reading for this book we became aware of a quest which scholars have quietly been pursuing over the centuries, the quest for the central mountain, which the Indians call Mount

Meru, and for the primal paradise around it. Sir Walter Raleigh in his *History of the World* identified the mountain as Ararat where Noah's Ark came to rest, but he located that peak far to the east of its actual site on the border of Turkey and Armenia. As geographical knowledge increased, successive newly found mountains were claimed as Meru. A popular candidate in the nineteenth century was the Pamir range in southern Turkestan to the north-east of Afghanistan. Its high, square plateau forms a plain around a central peak, and from it in different directions flow four great rivers. M.G. Maspero in *Histoire ancienne* was confident that there was to be found 'the navel of the world and the cradle of the human race'.

The moderns have succeeded in determining its site more definitely than the ancients were able to do. They have placed it in the mountains of the Belurtag, near the place where this chain unites with the Himalayas, upon the plateau of Pamir. There, in effect, and there alone, we find a country which satisfies all the descriptions, geographically speaking, preserved in the sacred books of Asia. From the plateau of Pamir, or better, the mountain mass of which this region is the central plain, four great rivers take their rise, the Indus, the Helmend, the Oxus, and the Jaxartes, which flow in directions the most diverse, well answering in this respect to the four rivers of sacred tradition.

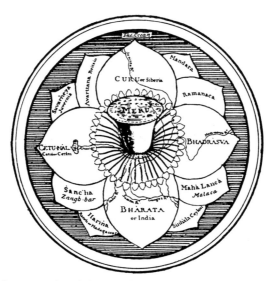

Fig. 14. The geography of the world with Meru at its centre is represented in Hindu Puranic symbolism as a 12-petalled lotus.

Fig. 15. Mount Kailas, the pyramid-shaped mountain which has the attributes of Meru, the mountain at the centre of the world.

In recent years mystical geographers have been inclined to look further east to a mountain which few western travellers had seen or heard of before the twentieth century. In western Tibet, just north of Nepal, is a mountain of remarkable appearance and reputation, Mount Kailas. Snow-clad and shaped like a towering, four-sided pyramid on a square platform, Kailas is of supreme sanctity to four religions, Hindu, Jain, Buddhist and the ancient Bon faith of Tibet. The depth of its lore, legend, history and associated ritual distinguishes it above all other mountains in the centre of the Asian continent. It is greatly revered as a place of pilgrimage. Until general access to it was blocked with the Communist takeover of Tibet, the paths between the five monasteries and numerous holy stations around it were walked by pilgrims from many nations. In his book about Kailas, *The Sacred Mountain*, the Buddhist John Snelling says:

47

It was the navel of the world, the seat of a sky goddess and the dwelling-place of 360 *Gi-kod*, a class of deity exclusive to Kailas and clearly associated with the year's turning. It was also down the 'heavenly cord' of Kailas that the emanation body of Shenrab, the founder of the formalized Bon religion, descended to earth. It was also imagined as a great *chorten* (or *stupa*) of rock crystal, and as a palace where several families of gods resided. It had four gates, one guarding each of the four cardinal points: Chinese tiger, tortoise, red bird and turquoise dragon.

Kailas further qualifies as the primary symbol of Mount Meru through the four major rivers, Indus, Sutlej, Brahmaputra and Karnali, which arise and flow outwards from its slopes.

If we suppose Kailas is the nearest thing on earth to Mount Meru, the question which follows is about the relationship between the actual mountain and its surroundings and the mythical world-axis at the centre of the former paradise. If Kailas is Meru, it is the place where God first made known the foundation law for all the 12-tribe nations which have ever since come into being. It is the source of human culture, and its shape and the features of its surroundings have been imitated in temples and symbolic land-scapes throughout the world. This idea of finding the original paradise on earth has a perennial attraction but, like all such quests, it requires a multi-dimensional approach. In our search for the true paradisial mountain which, so they say, is rooted in earth but extends to heaven above it and the underworld below, we are well guided by the methods described in René Daumal's story, *Mount Analogue*. It describes how a group of mystical mountain-eers use their knowledge of mythology, geography and esoteric psychology to create the type of reality which is necessary for their voyage to the mountain at the centre of the world.

In Daumal's subtle work is explored the puzzle which recurs throughout this book: that Mount Meru, the Soma drink of immortality which it conceals, the Holy Grail and the Garden of Paradise belong naturally to this earth and are sometimes apparent, but at other times they are withdrawn from sight. The difference between these two states, so mystics affirm, lies in human percep-tion. Thus we conceive of an ancient enchantment, created by a secret science of priestcraft, which placed the people of those 12-tribe nations who were subjected to it in a state of perception and spiritual intensity which coloured their lives with impressions of an earthly paradise.

48

5

The Celtic realm

THE SACRED GEOGRAPHY OF IRELAND

René Guénon in *Le Roi du monde*, published in 1927, seems to have been the first in modern times to draw attention to the hierarchical arrangement of the ancient Irish provinces round their meeting-place at an omphalos stone in the very centre of the country. The four existing provinces are Ulster in the north, Leinster in the east, Munster in the south and Connacht in the west. Formerly there was a central fifth province, Midhe (spelt, in English, as it is pronounced, Meath) which means Middle. It corresponded to Mediolanum, the central sanctuary of the Gauls. The symbolic function of Meath, as the fifth province which provides the point of balance between the other four, was formalized in about 130 AD when it was placed under the direct administration of the *ardri*, the high king of all Ireland. Thus it became at the same time a federal territory, a royal estate and a sacred precinct.

The lands of old Midhe comprised the two counties now called Meath and West Meath, together with parts of neighbouring counties. This central province contained the two principal institutions of traditional sacred government. In Meath is the old ritual centre, the Hill of Tara, and a spot in West Meath, the Hill of Uisnech, marks the geographic centre of Ireland.

The ancient significance of Tara is indicated by its legends and by the remains of a megalithic ritual chamber, a stone from which was the seat of the high king at his coronation. On the summit of the low, rounded hill, commanding extensive views over the landscape around, stood the great hall, designed as a microcosm of the whole kingdom. Therein, during the seasonal councils between the four provinces, the high king took his place at the centre, and around him, facing the directions of their respective

49

provinces, sat the four subsidiary kings. Their attendants and courtiers sat in hierarchical order in the four provincial halls on each side of the central building: the men of Ulster on the north side, Leinster to the east, Munster to the south and Connacht to the west. Through imitating the pattern of a perfectly ordered universe, the kings and nobles of Ireland symbolized the harmony which they hoped to achieve in their deliberations. The symbolic order, together with chanting and other Druidic arts, created the enchantment which maintained the high culture of old Ireland. Security was upheld on all levels, from the physical to the psychic. The high king united the country against invaders and demons alike. At the feast of Samain or Hallowe'en, when dead spirits and forces of evil are abroad, he took his place on the throne in the middle of the great hall, and the provincial kings sat enthroned at the four quarters with their retinues behind them – an arrangement which can be reproduced with a pack of playing cards.

This pattern is further described by Alwyn and Brinley Rees in their book *Celtic Heritage*. They point to other examples in ritual and cosmology of four units round a fifth, typified by the five *16b* sacred mountains of China, one of which is central and the others at the four points of the compass. This pattern is the basis of the

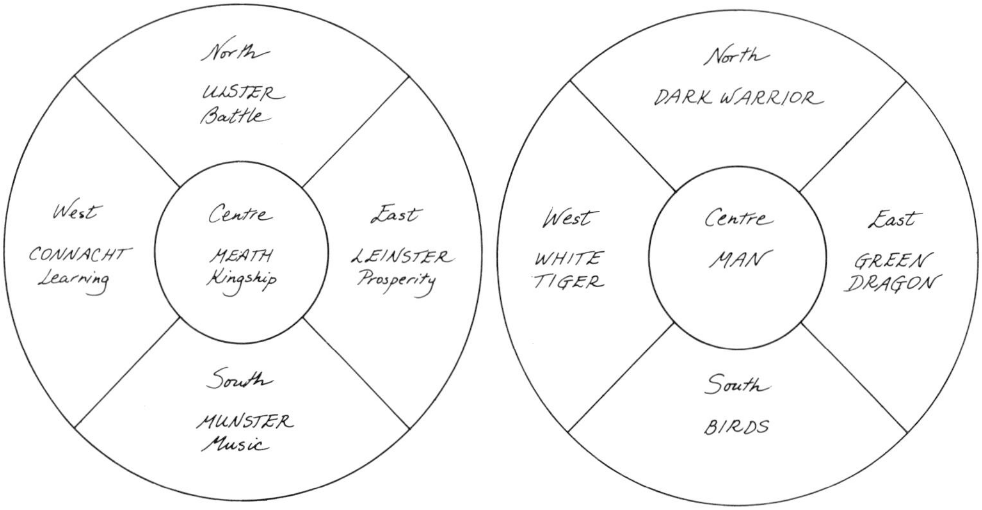

Fig. *16a and b*. The four provinces around Meath at the centre of ancient Ireland had many symbolic attributes. Their general characteristics, set out in the diagram above left, are comparable to those of the four quarters in Chinese cosmology (right).

Fig. 17. The prehistoric earthworks of the Hill of Tara enclosed the great hall and ritual centre of Ireland's high king, the place of assembly for the hierarchy of the four quarters.

traditional diagram behind all the ancient, cosmically ordered societies. From it naturally develops the familiar 12-fold order of courts and pantheons. As each of the four seasons has three months, so each of the four kings is flanked by two attendants and each of the four provinces is divided into three tribes. Twelve was the number of seats arranged round a king's throne in the royal halls of Ireland, as in the palace of King Conchobar of Ulster *16a* mentioned earlier; the king of Munster headed 12 lesser kings, and 12 kings, three from each province, attended the high king at his installation on the stone of Tara.

There were said to be 12 noble races in Ireland, as there were 12 lakes, 12 mountains, 12 winds and 12 rivers issuing from the omphalos stone at Uisnech. As a rule, there were three kings to *17* each province, one of them being superior, and below them was an elaborate network of lesser chiefs, each one an independent ruler, subject only to his superior in the same way that the provincial kings were subject to the high king at Tara. The same pattern ran throughout, every establishment from the provincial courts to the halls of tribal chiefs and individual dwellings being modelled on the exemplary hall of the high king, which was itself a reflection of the heavenly order.

About forty miles west of Tara is the Hill of Uisnech where the pillar stood which marked the geographical centre of Ireland, the crossing point of the boundary lines between the four provinces. Giraldus Cambrensis referred to it as the navel of Ireland. The Reeses quote an old Irish text which describes how, early in the Christian era, Fintan, the leading geomancer of Ireland, was commissioned to survey the island's divisions. After he had done so, he set up on the Hill of Uisnech a pillar stone with five ridges on it. 'And he assigned a ridge on it to every province in Ireland, for thus are Tara and Uisnech in Ireland, as its two kidneys are in a beast.'

These five provinces were not Meath and the four quarters, but Connacht, Leinster, Ulster and the two Munsters, thus indicating an alternative division of Ireland into five sectors from the central pillar. References to the two different systems have caused much scholarly confusion, but a study of the map of Ireland shows how the two were reconciled.

18a   The first map shows the old boundaries of the four Irish provinces. The boundaries themselves are ancient, though some of the counties have shifted allegiance in historical times. The county of Louth in north-east Leinster was for a time, between the reigns of King John and Elizabeth I, included in Ulster. Its coastal boundary is at the head of Carlingford Lough where it meets the two Ulster counties, Armagh and Down. County Clare has undergone several changes. Up to 1565 it was an independent kingdom, after which it was made part of Connacht. In Elizabeth's reign it was administered separately. Charles II placed it in Munster where it still is today, but it is cut off from Munster by the wide Shannon estuary which forms its southern border, and geographically it is part of Connacht. We locate its coastal boundary mark at the narrow entrance to the Shannon estuary, where Clare and the Munster county of Kerry are nearest to each other. It must also be remembered that the six counties which comprise Northern Ireland today do not represent the whole of Ulster, which properly includes Donegal.

When straight lines are drawn diagonally between the coastal

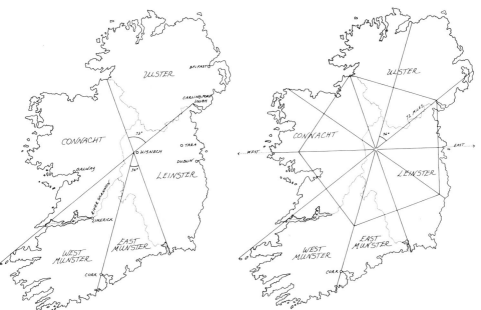

Fig. 18a. Lines drawn diagonally between the coastal boundary points of Ireland's four provinces meet to form angles of exactly 72 degrees. One of these angles is bisected by a line to the boundary mark between East and West Munster.

Fig. 18b. The due east-west line through the centre of Ireland fits into the pentagonal scheme of sacred geometry, which is suggested by the lines in the previous diagram. This prior division of the country into ten sectors from the symbolic centre develops into the 12-part division shown in the following diagram.

meeting-places of the four provinces, their point of intersection is found to be in West Meath, a short distance to the west of the traditional centre of Uisnech. From this point another line is drawn to the city of Cork at the head of Cork Harbour, the old boundary mark between East and West Munster.

From the second map it will be seen that these lines from the centre to the five coastal boundary markers are not at random angles, but indicate a regular ten-part division of a circle, each neighbouring pair of lines forming an angle of 36°. Within this scheme is an obvious pentagon. Three of its five radii are already marked, by the line dividing East and West Munster and by the lines to the two extreme boundary marks of Ulster. We note that these two marks are equidistant from the centre, seventy-two miles from it, and that 72° is the angle they form. This is the pentagonal angle, and a pentagon with its northern side drawn between the

18b

extremities of Ulster neatly covers the heart of Ireland. The word 'province' means a fifth part, and this pentagonal pattern may represent the earliest symbolic division of Ireland.

The longest of the ten dividing lines, running between the extreme eastern and western points of the country, cuts the island into two almost equal halves, as also does the other line between two provincial boundaries. Ireland is about 350 miles long from north to south and an average of 170 miles wide. Its shape is irregular, but an approximate quartering of its territory is achieved by this geomantic figure. The elongated provinces, Ulster in the north and Munster in the south, are each given two of the ten sectors, while three each are given to Leinster and Connacht whose lands do not extend so far from the centre.

This archaic division was adapted very simply to a 12-part zodiacal scheme by making both Ulster and Munster into three sectors. The traditions of all four provinces refer to their former tripartite divisions, so in the complete development of Ireland's sacred geography the ten-part division gives way to the twelve. There are no firm clues to the extent of Meath, the fifth province, traditionally made up of territory taken from the other four. In figure 18c we have suggested it by a circle passing through the Hill of Tara, which gives to all five provinces a roughly equal portion of habitable land, the extra territory of West Munster being largely barren.

There can be little doubt that this is how Fintan, and Druid geomancers centuries before him, surveyed the divisions of Ireland. Every line plays a part in defining the geographical extremities of the island or the coastal meeting-points of its provinces. Thus marked are the extreme eastern, western and southern points, the north-east corner and the inlets of several principal rivers. Identified *18c* by their letters on the map, the six pairs of lines mark the following features:

Line AG is remarkable in that it goes between the most eastern and the most western points of Ireland and also passes over the coastal junctions of Ulster with Leinster and of Munster with Connacht along the Shannon estuary. Its western terminus, the farthest rock of the Blasket Islands, also marks the extreme western point of Europe.

BH is the east-west baseline, dividing the country laterally into two halves. It goes from near to the westernmost point of mainland

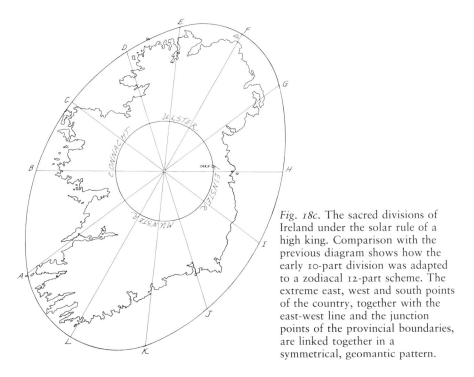

Fig. 18c. The sacred divisions of Ireland under the solar rule of a high king. Comparison with the previous diagram shows how the early 10-part division was adapted to a zodiacal 12-part scheme. The extreme east, west and south points of the country, together with the east-west line and the junction points of the provincial boundaries, are linked together in a symmetrical, geomantic pattern.

Connacht at Slyne Head, through the eastern extremity of Leinster at Lambay Island, and to the northernmost tip of Wales, the Skerries Rock off Anglesey.

CI has its western limit at Berowee Head, the north-west tip of County Mayo.

DJ marks at its south-eastern end the border between Leinster and Munster, where the rivers Barrow and Suir flow together into the estuary at Waterford Harbour. To the north-east it divides at the coast the counties of Donegal and Leitrim and the provinces of Ulster and Connacht.

EK runs between Youghal Bay in the south to the north of Ulster, but not its most northern point. This is the only extremity not linked to the system.

FL links the north-eastern tip of Ulster at Torr Head, the point of Ireland nearest to Scotland, with Ireland's southernmost rock, the Fastnet Rock beyond Cape Clear.

These divisions indicate a noble work of geomancy, uniting the whole of Ireland under the sacred 12-fold pattern. The lines take in the mouths and estuaries of important rivers, including the

Barrow, the Suir, the Blackwater and the Shannon, which form natural boundaries, as well as the principal headlands. Some overall figure of sacred geometry must have completed the design. The form which appears most likely is an oval mandorla, symbol of the virgin goddess whom the high king of Ireland ceremonially married at his coronation.

This figure is also the world-egg of Druid cosmology. Fabre d'Olivet, writing on the traditional science behind music, took the egg to represent the union of two strings of unequal length, which express the full range of harmonies in the music of the spheres. In his *Music Explained as Science and Art* he concluded that 'the Universe is by no means contained, as the vulgar seem to think, in a perfect circle, but in a sort of oval, which the Orphics rightly depicted in the form of an egg...'

THE ANCIENT DIVISIONS OF WALES

Like Ireland, Wales was also at one time divided into five provinces, one of them lying at the centre of the other four. Its thirteen ancient counties (including Monmouth which is now improperly part of England) can be seen as the traditional pattern of 12 round a thirteenth, and the number 12 framed many of its old institutions. There is indeed an early reference to the division of Wales into the classical four quarters and 12 tribal areas. William of Malmesbury, in the fourth chapter of his twelfth-century *History of Glastonbury*, quotes an earlier book, *The Deeds of the Ancient Britons*, where it says that 12 brothers from the north of Britain came down to Wales to take possession of their ancestral estates. Their lands consisted of four territories: Gwynned, Dyfed, Gower and Kidwelly. The names of the 12 brothers were: Ludnerth, Morgen, Catgur, Cathmor, Merguid, Morvined, Morehel, Morcant, Boten, Morgent, Mortineil and Glasteing.

The old boundaries of Wales have constantly been disturbed by strife and invasions. Romans, Saxons, Normans and neighbours from Scotland, Ireland and England have at different times ruled over the whole or parts of the country, obliterating much of its original geomantic pattern. Yet certain features of that pattern remain intact, providing clues for the following tentative reconstruction of the sacred divisions of ancient Wales.

19 The centre of Wales is mostly rugged highland, a meeting-place

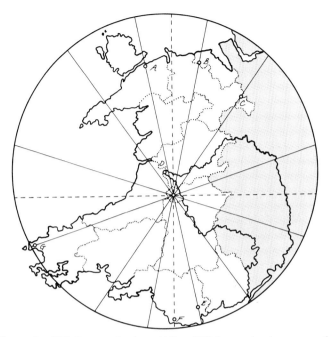

Fig. 19. The peak of Plinlimmon in the middle of Wales marks the centre of a circle which contains the whole country. From the lost tribal centre at Cwmdeuddwr lines drawn to the cathedral sites of Wales's four quarters conform to the same pattern as is found in the divisions of ancient Ireland. Other lines in the scheme are directed towards ancient sites of perpetual choirs, to the boundary mark with England and to the farthest headlands of the south and west coasts. The map shows the following sites:

A   Bangor.   D   Plinlimmon.   F   Llantwit Major.
B   St Asaph's.   E   Llandaff.   G   St David's.
C   Bangor-Is-Coed. ·

for the rivers and mountain ranges which form the natural boundaries of the four outlying provinces. These were the territories of the four distinct tribes of the Cymry encountered by the Romans. The four tribes retained their separate identities into Christian times, and the ecclesiastical division of Wales into four sees, each with its cathedral, was roughly in accordance with the previous arrangement. The divisions are:

North-west: Anglesey and the Snowdonia district. This was the land of the Decangi people. The cathedral is at Bangor.

North-east: Denbigh, Flint and parts of Montgomery and Merioneth, the land of the Ordovices, with its cathedral at St Asaph.

South-west: Cardigan, Carmarthen and Pembroke. The tribe were the Dimetae, the cathedral is at St David's.

South-east: Glamorgan, Monmouth, Brecknock and part of Radnor formed Siluria, the country of the Silures. The cathedral is at Llandaff.

Each of these tribal lands was ruled by a dynasty of kings, with a ritual court which included a chief justice, a high priest and a national bard. There were three lesser kingdoms or realms to each of the four quarters, making the traditional 12 divisions, and these were further subdivided into cantrefs or hundreds, commots and family holdings. The commots were supposed to be made up of fifty landed families, and each had its courthouse and place of assembly. Twice a year the king and his retainers made a ceremonial journey round all the provincial courts and assemblies, spending three days at each. In Glamorgan, and probably elsewhere throughout Wales, the king presided over a judicial council of 12 elders. According to the traditional genealogy of the kings of Glamorgan, recorded among the *Iolo Manuscripts*, this was instituted by Morgan Mwynfawr, the first of his dynasty. The custom of appointing 12 justices was long lasting in that part of Wales. It was followed by King Edgar in the tenth century when he appointed 12 judges to settle disputes in Glamorgan, and later the Normans administered the district through 12 knights in accordance with local practice. It has been suggested that the convention of 12 men to a jury has its origin in old Welsh law.

The fifth, central province of Wales was the Land between Two Rivers, referring to the Severn and Wye, both of which rise on the *20, 21* slopes of Plinlimmon mountain. The Welsh name of this mountain, Pumlumon, means five-peaked. In their *Celtic Heritage* Alwyn and Brinley Rees identify it as the old symbolic centre of the country, corresponding to the five-ridged stone on the Hill of Uisnech or the five-peaked central mountain of China. The highest point on the Plinlimmon range can indeed be called the centre of Wales. Figure 19 shows how a circle drawn from this point contains the extremities of the country and defines its natural geographical borders, the estuary of the Mersey to the north-east and the course of the Severn to the south-east.

A few miles to the south-east of Plinlimmon is a district which suggests itself as the ritual centre of ancient Wales. It is the legendary heart of the country, a region more or less encompassed

Fig. 20. Cwmdeuddwr, the wild district in the heart of Wales, is an administrative anomaly and forms a little country on its own. Ringed by hills and approached by ancient trackways, this spot is the theoretic centre of the four quarters and twelve tribal lands of Welsh sacred geography.

by a circle of four miles radius, which has always been regarded as a strange land on its own. Even today it is an administrative anomaly, forming a separate parish within Radnorshire, yet entirely cut off from the rest of the country by the river Wye to the east. Its name, Cwmdeuddwr, refers to the two rivers, the Wye and the Elan, which border it. Its once sacred valleys are today flooded by the reservoirs which give water to Birmingham, and many of its old relics and habitations lie beneath them. It remains a place of awesome atmosphere, where the powers of nature brood darkly.

The ancient sanctity of Cwmdeuddwr is evident in the megalithic circles, rows and standing stones across its mountains and the old tracks that converge upon it. In Celtic times it was a sanctuary of the Druids, fiercely defended against the Romans. Celtic saints of early Christianity formed settlements in its valleys, and were succeeded there by communities of medieval monks. On either side of Cwmdeuddwr, to the east and west, were two great religious houses, at Abbey-Cwmhir and Strata Florida. Their white-robed monks would process from one to the other, following an ancient path over the Cwmdeuddwr hills, chanting as they walked. The wild spirit of nature, which attracted hermits and holy men, made it a resort of poets, notably Shelley, and it gained early fame among tourists as having the most picturesque scenery in Wales.

Throughout Welsh history Cwmdeuddwr has been a place of last refuge. The British chieftain, Vortigern, was hunted down and killed there; Llewellyn, the last Welsh king, made it the centre of his resistance to the English until his defeat and death nearby in 1282, after which Edward I stripped the area of its forests as far as Strata Florida; it was also the stronghold of Owain Glyndwr during his guerrilla campaign in the early fifteenth century. For many years afterwards it was a domain of Welsh patriots and outlaws, where strangers rarely entered. Ancient customs and traditions, forgotten elsewhere, lingered there into modern times. Today it is a sanctuary for the native wildlife, the red kite and rare species of plants.

Cwmdeuddwr was probably the core of the fifth Welsh province between the other four, the realm of a former high king. The sacred geography of Wales, as indicated by the positions of the principal shrines of the four provinces, has its centre in the very heart of the district. A natural hillock on the west bank of the modern Craig Goch reservoir, where it is fed by the Cletwr brook, is the theoretic spot. Surrounded on all sides by an even ring of mountains, it strikes the imagination as a place for bardic and legislative assemblies. There or thereabouts is most likely to have been situated the annual congress of the 12 tribes of old Wales.

Figure 19 shows the likely pattern of symbolic geometry behind the divisions of ancient Wales. In shape Wales is roughly similar to Ireland, and both are naturally divided into two halves, north and south. These may once have had a symbolic male (north), female (south) relationship. The dimensions of Wales, its length and average width, are roughly half those of Ireland, but the same diagram applies to both countries. From a centre within Cwmdeuddwr, the above-mentioned Druid sanctuary, lines are drawn to the sites of the four cathedrals. The straight line between Bangor Cathedral in the north-west and Llandaff in the south-east passes right through the centre. The other two cathedrals are not so related, but lines to them from the centre produce angles which coincide with those in the Irish diagram (figure 18c). When the diagram is completed, its conformity to the boundaries and headlands of Wales becomes evident.

Fig. 21. Plinlimmon, the five-peaked mountain at the centre of Wales.

This is a circle of enchantment. The sacred places which are linked with the centre by the spokes of the wheel are the sites of ancient choirs. Three such are mentioned in an old Welsh Triad as 'perpetual choirs', where parties of monks chanted in unbroken succession, day and night and throughout the year. One of the choirs was at Llantwit Major near the south coast, where the learned St Illtyd founded a monastic college in the sixth century. It was called Bangor Illtyd, 'Bangor' meaning 'Fair Choir'. The main axis of the diagram, the line from Wales's northern promontory at Orm's Head to its southernmost bulge, passes through Illtyd's Choir.

The figure 2400, the number of saints at each of the three main perpetual choirs of Britain, recurs in the legend of St Illtyd's church foundations. In the *Iolo Manuscripts* is written, 'Illtyd founded seven churches, and appointed seven companies for each church, and seven halls or colleges in each company, and seven saints for each hall or college. And prayer and praise were kept up, without ceasing, day and night, by twelve saints, men of learning in each company.'

The total number of saints in the seven churches was therefore $7 \times 7 \times 7 \times 7 = 2401$, one more than the 2400 members of a perpetual choir. In this way the spiritual number seven, the number of days in a week, was combined with the number of hours in a day or of months in a year, the number twelve.

The cathedrals at St David's and St Asaph were also Celtic foundations and would thus have held choirs and chanting choristers. Another Bangor, near to which one of the lines is directed, is Bangor-is-coed, near Wrexham in the north-east quarter. It was the site of a Celtic choir, destroyed by Saxon invaders, which may have been one of the three perpetual choirs mentioned in the Triad.

As well as linking six principal choir sites in Wales, the diagram sends lines to three main promontories: the western extremity of the land at St David's Head and Ramsay Island beyond it; Worm's Head at the end of the Gower peninsula on the south coast, which is the far western point of Glamorgan and the south-eastern quarter of the country; Lavernock Point below Llandaff, which forms the south-eastern corner of Wales. The line to Worm's Head continues straight over Lundy Island in the Bristol Channel to Land's End in Cornwall. Also marked by one of the lines is the old border between Wales and England, at the mouth of the river Wye where Monmouthshire and Gloucestershire meet.

This pattern must be older than Christianity, but the use of so many of its key points as the choirs of Celtic Christianity suggests that the early Christians preserved knowledge of it from their Druid predecessors. The legendary days of sacred rule, when a nationwide system of perpetual choirs enthralled the whole country, were in the remote past. State Druidism in Wales was destroyed by the Romans, and by the beginning of the Christian era the old choirs had no doubt been silenced. With the Celtic saints came a musical as well as a spiritual revival. Lapsed choirs were restored, and the ancient spell was renewed with Christian plainchant.

Some idea of the elaborately ritualized society of Druidic Wales is conveyed by the system of traditional land measures which was designed to express the tribal order. The definitions of these measures were confirmed in the code of Welsh law which King Howel the Good established at the beginning of the tenth century. It was based entirely on ancient precedents. In accordance with custom, Howel appointed a committee of 12 jurists, presided over by a doctor of law, to reassemble the traditional laws and standards of the country. Their information on land measures provides a rare glimpse of the esoteric code behind the institutions of Druidism.

The smallest, family landholding was an allotment of 4 acres. Of these there were 64 in a clan, a practically self-sufficient group which was based on an extensive farmstead. Four farmsteads made up a maenol, an association of neighbours, and there were many further divisions, as listed below. In every unit a portion of the land was set aside for various public purposes, for the ruler, for the old and indigent and as a tithe to the Druids. This is reflected in the definition of a commot, which consisted either of 50 farmsteads or of 12 maenols plus two farmsteads, those two being for the king's use. The number system behind these divisions is evidently the same traditional model, framed by the number 12, which formed the structure of 12-tribe societies everywhere. Thus there were 12 'realms' in ancient Wales, three to each quarter and corresponding roughly to the present counties. Each was of 120 square miles, and 1440 square miles was the measure of the entire country.

4 acres = 1 allotment (*tyddyn*)
4 allotments = 16 acres = 1 *rander*
16 allotments = 64 acres = 1 *garael*
64 allotments = 256 acres = 1 farmstead (*trev*)
4 farmsteads = 1024 acres = 1 *maenol*
50 farmsteads = 12,800 acres = 1 commot (*cwmwd*)
100 farmsteads = 25,600 acres = 1 cantref
3 cantrefs = 120 square miles = 1 realm
3 realms = 360 square miles = 1 quarter
4 quarters = 1440 square miles = sacred Wales

The actual size of Wales, including its extensive mountains and wildernesses, is about five times larger than the symbolic 1440 square miles, but that area represents roughly the amount of Welsh land that can be cultivated. More essentially, this use of number indicates the overall nature of the society to which it was applied. The 1440 square miles of sacred Wales correspond numerically to the 1440 acres within the square borders of St John's New Jerusalem (figure 25) and to the 1440 acres which formed the legendary 12 hides of Glastonbury (a hide is 120 acres). They are the measure of paradise as represented in traditional cosmology. In some distant period, certainly before Christianity, the tribes of Wales received a law, the same law which has been received at different times by peoples throughout the world, a law based on the ideal image of the cosmos, numerically expressed and enacted principally through music. The sacred divisions of Wales were a product of that law.

TWELVE SAINTS AND THE ENCHANTMENTS OF BRITAIN

A zodiacal circle, formed by 12 knights, saints, hermits or mission-aries, is a recurrent image in old British legends. Like the Grail, it is associated with periods of regeneration and sacred order, when the countryside is prosperous and life is experienced on a high level of spiritual intensity. At such a time King Arthur set up his Round Table, a model of the divine cosmos, as the central symbol in his court of 12 knights, each representing a zodiacal constellation. This event belongs to no single age or locality, for relics of an Arthurian myth cycle occur in local traditions and place names in Celtic landscapes from Scotland to Brittany. Many different towns and hilltops have claims to have been Camelot, Arthur's citadel, and no doubt many of these claims are justified, for the 12-part story of Arthur and his companions appears to have been established and celebrated throughout the year by the various Celtic tribes or tribal unions within their own territories.

Medieval chroniclers told of the enchantments of Britain, and behind their tales of adventurous or culture-bearing heroes can be detected a theme of revival through missionary groups, often twelve in number, who aspired to re-create that former state of enchantment, when initiated bards by their musical arts held earthly life in tune with the harmony of the heavens.

The most famous story is of St Joseph of Arimathaea's mission. Shortly after the Crucifixion he and eleven companions were sent by the Apostle, St Philip, to establish Christianity in Britain. They reached Glastonbury, which was then an island hill surrounded by the Somerset lakes and marshes, and on one of its peaks, Wirral or Weary-all hill, St Joseph planted his staff. It grew to become the first of the Glastonbury thorn trees, which blossom at Christ-mastide. The local ruler gave St Joseph an area of land amounting to 12 hides, one hide or 120 acres for each member of his party,

Fig. 22. King Arthur's Round Table, now exhibited in the castle of Winchester, commemorates the aspirations of successive English kings to revive through their dynasties the enchanted realm of Celtic legend. The oak table, eighteen feet in diameter, originally stood on twelve legs. It is divided into twelve white and twelve green sectors, each bearing the name of a Celtic noble, and at the head is a portrait of Henry VIII. The table was made earlier, probably in the thirteenth-century reign of Edward I, who modelled himself and his court on the Arthurian ideal.

and at its centre the missionaries built a simple church, surrounded by 12 huts in which they dwelt.

Another of Glastonbury's legends tells of a second foundation, also by 12 holy men. During the second century, in the reign of King Lucius, a missionary party, led by two priests, Deruvian and Phagan, came to Britain from Rome and found at Glastonbury the remains of St Joseph's original settlement. They also found a written account of its history. This caused them to restore the ancient church and to appoint twelve of their number as its ministers. The twelve lived as hermits in secluded places around Glastonbury, and whenever one of them died a new hermit was elected in his place, so the number was always maintained. This went on until 433, the traditional date of St Patrick's arrival in

Glastonbury. The names of the 12 hermits at that time are given in the thirteenth-century St Patrick's Charter as:

Brumban, Hyregaan, Brenwal, Wencreth, Bantommeweng, Adelwalred, Lothor, Wellias, Breden, Swelwes, Hinloernus and Hin.

These strangely named individuals were organized into a religious community by St Patrick, who thus became the first abbot at Glastonbury. After his death in 472, his relics attracted many Irish pilgrims to Glastonbury.

Scotland, Wales, Cornwall and Gaul were also evangelized during the sixth century by groups of 12 holy men. St Columba had 12 companions when he left Ireland to found the monastery at Iona at the start of his Scottish mission. His near-namesake and fellow Irishman, St Columban, brought Celtic Christianity to Gaul with the assistance of 12 monks. They settled as hermits in the Vosges mountains and were responsible for the renewal of culture and prosperity which followed. St Gall, Columban's successor, led 12 disciples to a new settlement in Switzerland.

Another 12 holy anchorites formed the first Christian church in Wales, in about 56 AD according to the legend. It was at or near Llantwit Major on the south coast. They were assembled by St Eurgain, the wife of Caradoc or Caractacus who fought against the Romans. As leader of the community, she appointed St Ilid, a Jew from Rome. Early in the sixth century his foundation was reformed by the learned St Illtyd, who made the place into one of the greatest centres of education in Europe. The Welsh chieftains were proud to send their children there, and the conversion of Wales was thus accomplished by the force of enlightenment.

A similar pattern of events is recorded in the life of St Petroc, the patron saint of Cornwall. He purified that country by banishing an evil monster which had been devastating it, and then retired to the wilderness of Bodmin Moor, where he settled with 12 fellow hermits. The magical influence of St Petroc and his 12 followers is indicated by one of his legends. It tells how the saint struck a rock with his staff and a spring welled up, transforming the waste into a fertile countryside and bringing in an age of prosperity. Another mission to Cornwall was that of St Paul or Paulinus, who led 12 presbyters from Carmarthenshire in Wales to the court of Cornwall's King Mark, and then proceeded to Brittany.

The most important group of 12 Celtic saints were the Twelve Apostles of Ireland who, early in the sixth century, formed a college for the administration of religious affairs under the great St Finnian of Clonard in Meath. Following the missionary work of St Patrick and his contemporaries, St Finnian reorganized the Church in Ireland on more formal lines. He founded or reformed the monastery at Clonard to be a centre of education and law. Each of his followers were heads of similar establishments in different parts of the country, and together they made up an authoritative body which in some ways corresponded to the amphictyonic council of Delphi some thousand years earlier. In both cases the main responsibility of the twelve was to manage and protect the priestly estates and to uphold the rights of sanctuary. The names of the Apostles and their principal foundations were:

Ciaran the elder of Saighir

Ciaran the younger of Clonmacnois

Columba or Columcille, founder of several monasteries in Ireland and, with 12 followers, on the island of Iona

Brendan the Navigator, founder of Clonfert, who is thought by some to have sailed as far as America and to have preached there

Brendan of Birr

Colman or Columba of Terryglass

Molaisse of Devenish Island

Canice of Aghaboe in Ossory

Ruadan of Lorrha

Mobi the flat-faced of Glasnevin

Sinnel of Cluaininnis

Nannid of Inis mac Saint

Earlier in this chapter we described the sacred geography of Ireland and its government by 12 tribal rulers under a high king. This pattern was perpetuated by the early Church. It was customary, when a local king converted to Christianity, for the missionary saint to build a church and monastery on the site of the main tribal sanctuary, where formerly the Druid priests had officiated. From the people of the tribe came the first monks and priests, many of whom were evidently former Druids or pupils from their colleges. It seems therefore that Christianity brought little change to the social order, and even the forms of religion were not radically altered. So much of the native tradition was preserved and incorporated by the early Church that one may reasonably view the Twelve Apostles of Ireland as ecclesiastical representatives of Ireland's traditional 12 tribes. St Finnian in that case would have taken on the authority of a former Chief Druid of Ireland, attached to the court of the high king and guiding the 12 chief priests of the provinces.

There is another hint of a circle of 12 sacred places in the life of St David, who is credited with having founded 12 monasteries across southern England and Wales. The list of these places includes Glastonbury where Christianity was established before David's time. There and probably elsewhere he reformed and enlarged an existing sanctuary. This implies that the legend of his 12 foundations has a symbolic meaning, its underlying reference being the traditional 12-spoked wheel of sanctity, the ancient model for a heavenly order on earth.

This 12-fold pattern is deeply rooted in Celtic mythology and the Grail legend. King Arthur fought 12 battles, conquered 12 kingdoms and slew the 12 kings of Orkney, whom Merlin then commemorated by a monument with 12 effigies. In the Grail romances, Sir Galahad is said to have founded the order of the Holy Grail, appointing 12 knights as guardians of the Round Table which St Joseph first established in Britain. St Joseph's sister bore 12 children to the Celtic hero, Bran, and another group of 12 saints, including St David's mother St Non, were the offspring of Brychan, a fifth-century king of Brecon. In the *High History of the Holy Grail* are named 12 brother knights, one of whom, Alain, was Percival's ancestor. They possessed 12 castles corresponding to the zodiacal signs.

When these fragments of old lore are pieced together, an overall picture emerges. A disenchanted wasteland is settled by 12 holy men who live as hermits around a central shrine. Through their influence the wilderness is made fertile, and some time later the pattern of their original settlement is magically reproduced across the whole country by a circle of 12 great monasteries around a national sanctuary. So we are told, both in the Grail legends and in the early lore of the Celtic Church, but in all such accounts there is a missing ingredient. We are never told just how this development occurred, how a circle of 12 humble hermits expanded to encompass an entire people and countryside.

A key to the mystery is found in the most distinctive possession of the Celtic Church, its musical tradition. Wherever the Celtic missionaries settled, their first concern was to build a simple oratory at the centre of their ring of cells. There they kept a

Fig. 23. The legend of King Arthur and his twelve knights preserves the memory of zodiacal, twelve-tribe division of all Celtic territories. Regular gatherings of the twelve knights or tribal chiefs first took place in forest sanctuaries, as depicted in Gustave Doré's nineteenth-century engraving.

ceaseless vigil, succeeding each other in turn throughout the hours of day and night, and at the same time they maintained a perpetual sacred chant. A chant is an intonation for the weaving of a spell. It is the most powerful ally of priestcraft, and its potential was clearly recognized by the Celtic Christians, for during the whole history of their Church, from the earliest times to the days of grand monasteries and abbeys, every community upheld a perpetual chant and lived under the spell of sacred music. Even in the seventh century, not many years before the Celtic Church was disestablished at the Synod of Whitby, St Aidan of Lindisfarne chose 12 boys from among his pupils to be his apostles in the evangelizing of northern England. These 12 were probably among other things Aidan's chief choristers.

In the many stories of how Christianity was brought to various parts of Britain and other countries by bands of 12 saintly hermits one can detect a musical undertone. The Celtic Church in Britain drew its traditions from the East rather than from Rome, and the greatest asset of the eastern Church is the canon of music and chanting which is said to have been adapted from the temple music of ancient Egypt. The temple chant was astrologically arranged in 12 parts under the 12 zodiacal signs and months of the year. It was performed by 12 master choristers, each one the leader of his own choir. Their musical tradition was inherited and revived by the early Church. Missionary groups of 12 brought the sacred chant to many countries, and the legends of Britain testify to its early appearance in these islands.

Yet the art of enchantment through music was not alien to Britain, for the Druids also maintained perpetual choirs. Modern historians are inclined to regard the early Celtic Church as a reformation of Druidism, the change of religion being largely a matter of adopting new names and symbols. Such a reformation may have been due by astrological reckoning, for the Celtic Church is unique in claiming no martyrs and little is heard of Druid opposition to the new faith. A change in music, the adoption of a new chant for the new era, must have played an important part in the transition from Druidism to Christianity. It may well be that the main attraction of Christianity, and the gift which the legendary groups of 12 missionaries spread throughout early Christendom, was the promise of a renewed musical enchantment through the 12-part plainchant of 12 evangelizing choristers.

As music was given an astrological framework, so also were landscapes. Wherever is found the legend of 12 saints or heroes who sanctified their surroundings, there one may look for an ancient sacred landscape, divided into 12 astrological segments.

Each segment had its peculiar symbols, music and myth, representing a twelfth part of the astrological circle and the cycles of music and mythology which had been adopted for the country as a whole. The pattern was laid out round the tribal or national sanctuary, such as was Glastonbury to the tribes of ancient Somerset; and Glastonbury retains the memory of a former astrological landscape in the story of its 12 saintly founders who each received a hide, or 120 acres of land. William of Malmesbury in the twelfth century said that the place of St Joseph's foundation 'may rightly be called an heavenly sanctuary upon earth', and that the old church 'savoured somewhat of heavenly sanctity ... and exhaled it over the whole country'. A site of such ancient and constant sanctity, a centre of the Arthurian mythic cycle and the Celtic mysteries, and with many other sacred and astrological associations; such a place proclaims itself as the location of a former zodiacal circle; and there is indeed the suggestion of an ancient circle of zodiacal figures, laid out across the landscape around Glastonbury.

The Glastonbury Zodiac, a product of nature, human efforts *24* and the imagination combined, was recognized in the summer of 1929 by a young artist, Kathryn Maltwood, who was engaged at the time in illustrating an edition of the *High History of the Holy Grail*, translated from the old French *Perceval le Gallois ou le conte du Graal*. The writer of this book stated that its origin was a Latin manuscript, 'taken in the Isle of Avalon, in a holy house of religion that standeth at the head of the Moors Adventurous, there where King Arthur and Queen Guinevere lie' – evidently meaning the library of Glastonbury Abbey. Maltwood discerned the astrological framework behind the adventures of Perceval, Arthur and the other characters in the Grail quest, and was struck by the idea that the whole story might be localized within the Glastonbury landscape. One evening, looking out from a Glastonbury hill over the flat countryside towards Cadbury hill, the locally claimed site of King Arthur's Camelot, she noticed in the shadows moving across the landscape the outlines of gigantic effigy figures. From the study of maps and aerial photographs she identified a circle about ten miles in diameter containing 12 astrological effigies, delineated by the shape of hills, streams and other landscape features. Their relative positions were in accordance with a map of the constellations, and there appeared to be references to some of the figures in local place names and folklore.

In her writings on the Glastonbury Zodiac, Kathryn Maltwood gave astronomical reasons for suggesting that the figures were formed about 5000 years ago, through artificial improvements to natural landscape shapes, by a people from the East, perhaps the

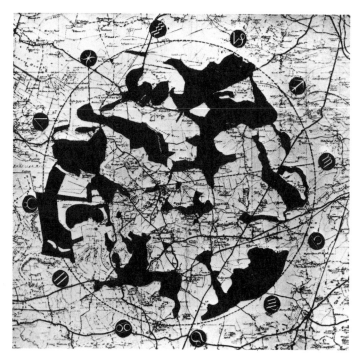

Fig. 24. The zodiacal figures which Kathryn Maltwood picked out
on the Somerset landscape.

Sumerians who might have given their name to Somerset. Around
the zodiacal figures had accumulated the episodes in the Grail
quest, and the complete circle was an image of the Round
Table, an emblem of the Celtic mysteries. Maltwood's *Guide to
Glastonbury's Temple of the Stars* began with a quotation from
La Queste del Saint Graal:

The Round Table was constructed, not without great significance, upon
the advice of Merlin. By its name the Round Table is meant to signify
the round world and round canopy of the planets and the elements in
the firmament, where are to be seen the stars and many other things.

This could indeed be a reference to a work of landscape sculpture
on the scale of the proposed Glastonbury Zodiac. The Maltwood
thesis has attracted enthusiasts and scoffers alike, but there is a
certain propriety about it which appeals to many discerning people.
The great esoteric scholar, René Guénon, in his long review of *A
Guide to Glastonbury's Temple of the Stars*, observed astrological

features of the Zodiac which, he said, 'may be regarded as marks of its authenticity', and concluded that 'the main part of the book, with the maps that bear out its theme, can not easily be set aside as purely fantastic'. He regarded favourably the author's belief that the secret of the zodiacal circle had been transmitted through the Druids to the monks of Glastonbury Abbey, and had also been preserved by the Knights Templar. This, he wrote, 'would harmonize the Templars' supposed connection with the Knights of the Round Table, and with the role of "Guardians of the Grail", attributed to them'.

We reproduce (figure 24) the circle of effigies as Kathryn Maltwood pictured them. Her modern followers, notably Mary Caine who has produced a film and a book on the Glastonbury Zodiac, have suggested amendments to some of the figures, while affirming belief in the general rightness of Maltwood's vision. As Guénon implied, it is hard to dismiss out of hand an image of such poetic strength. The evidence throughout this book shows that the ancients did indeed create landscapes on an astrological pattern. It was indeed the practice to attach episodes in the tribal mythology to hills and other landscape features, which were often seen as figurative representations of mythological characters, corresponding to the heavenly bodies. The Glastonbury Zodiac is thus a powerful and haunting symbol, evoking ancient memories. Since Kathryn Maltwood's time its effigies have been tended and preserved by her local followers, and the concept of a landscape zodiac is now established in many minds. Whether or not she was right in her interpretation of it, her perception of an astrological pattern at Glastonbury is well founded and effective. It points the way towards appreciating the scale on which the ancients applied the emblems of esoteric science to the sanctification of entire landscapes.

6

The cosmological foundation of twelve-tribe kingdoms

Behind all the foregoing examples of 12-tribe societies which have arisen at different times and places about the world, there is one original model. The pattern which they all imitate is the slowly revolving zodiac in the heavens, divided into 12 sectors or houses under 12 constellations, and traversed by 7 wandering luminaries, the sun, the moon, Mercury, Mars, Venus, Jupiter and Saturn.

The 7 moving lights are natural creations, and nature has also provided the 7 colours of the rainbow, the 7-day phase of the moon and the 7 notes of the diatonic musical scale. In the language of symbolism, the Septenary, which is rarely manifest in physical nature, represents the movement of spirit. It therefore specially pertains to the primordial stage of society, when small groups of people wandered like the planets around their native territory.

With the beginning of civilization, the number 12 rose naturally to prominence. That number is the proper foundation of a sacred order, for the laws of creation are mathematical, and the influence of the number 12, which provides the framework of number itself, has produced an essentially duodecimal universe. With that understanding, founders and reformers of civilization have constantly detected a 12-part pattern in the heavens, and have brought that pattern to earth in the form of zodiacal landscapes and 12-tribe societies.

These cosmic constitutions have differed from each other in many details, according to the nature of the people and countries they were applied to, but they have all been based on a traditional formula, a numerical cosmology which contains and codifies all the proportions and harmonies by which the universe was created. The revelation of that formula, and its adoption as the ruling standard throughout society, brought earthly life into harmony with the order and rhythm of the heavens, and made the conditions which are referred to poetically as the golden age.

Describing the ideal cosmological order in his *Laws*, Plato said that societies based on its formula will last as long as their foundation law is scrupulously maintained. They can not, however, be eternal, for even the best-founded civilizations are subject to the law of mortality which appoints an end to every material structure. Either by foreign invasion or internal corruption every ideal constitution is finally dissolved. Yet the foundation formula, though it may at times seem lost and forgotten, is not subject to mortality, for it is not physical but archetypal. It is inherently present in nature and the human mind, and its various symbols – Elysium, the Grail, the plan of the heavenly city or cosmic temple – have been the objects of repeated quests by individuals, groups and movements dedicated to the restoration of sacred order. The work has been approached from many different angles by people of very different casts of mind: scholars and visionaries, musicians and warriors, Pythagorean geometers, initiates of the mystery schools, alchemists, Rosicrucians, freemasons, cabalists and Crusaders. Some have had access to parts of the old tradition, while others have sought it through inspiration. In every period of renaissance and millennial fervour, minds have been stirred by the recurring image of celestial government on earth.

Western literature has two famous examples of the ancient cosmological formula, depicted in both cases as an ideal city. They were recorded by two men of apparently dissimilar mentalities. Plato, with his politician's mind, presented his model as a practical guide to the reconstitution of those 12-tribe amphictyonies which had previously obtained among all the peoples of Greece. St John the Divine, a visionary scholar, described his city as a 12-faceted pattern in the heavens, descending to earth as the New Jerusalem, where the twelve tribes of Israel would reassemble in the light of Christian revelation. These two cities are essentially one and the same, for they are based on the same model. By studying its given dimensions we can reconstruct the numerical and geometric form of that model, and therein appears the foundation plan of traditional 12-tribe societies in every part of the world.

PLATO'S AMPHICTYONY

Plato was born in 427 BC and died at the age of eighty. He lived at a time when the 12-tribe amphictyonies and the sacred landscapes of archaic Greece were in a state of decay and dissolution. Plato was an initiate of the Egyptian and other mystery schools, and it is clear from his writings that he understood the mathematical formula behind the traditional cosmology and meant to use his knowledge to promote the reconstruction of ideal societies on the ancient model. His political career was a fiasco due to the intransigence of the Sicilian king whom he tried to influence. But in his books, though often in veiled or allegorical form, he left a complete guide to the old esoteric science. The reason for his occasional obscurity, which he employs when important matters are being discussed, was to preserve sacred knowledge from those who were not adapted to benefit themselves or others by it. Behind the outward form of his ideal amphictyonic state, which he described in the *Laws* under the name Magnesia, lies a cosmological scheme of number, proportion and music, known only to initiates. Plato refers to this scheme by one of the symbolic numbers which feature in it, the number 5040. This is the proposed number of citizens in Magnesia, and it is applied to all other institutions of the state.

Magnesia's outward form and constitution reproduce, probably in quite accurate detail, those of the old amphictyonies in their early days, before corruption set in, when life was innocent and rule was by simple principles, enunciated through music. This was the state which Plato wished to restore. He proposed the foundation of a new, 12-tribe, 5040-citizen colony which, he promised, would last almost for ever if the laws he framed for it were strictly maintained.

His first concern was the overall geomancy of the site of the colony. Its climate, the direction of its prevailing winds, the quality of its waters and the nutriments in its soil must be tested, and it is also important to ascertain what sort of influence the land is likely to have on the characters of people born there. In this consideration Plato resembles a Chinese geomancer. His prescription of an ideal site is, 'where the winds of heaven blow, where spirits possess the land and greet kindly, or unkindly, the various sorts of people who settle in it'.

The site should not be too near the sea, where the citizens would be exposed to the corrupting influence of seafaring traders. Once located, it should be hallowed by various rituals. Its sacred places should be sought out and reconsecrated. Festivals should be held there at appropriate dates so that there are not less than 365 festivals during the course of the year.

As near as possible in the centre of the country, says Plato, is to be the acropolis and national shrine, enclosed by a wall and dedicated to a divine trinity, Hestia, Zeus and Athena. Around it is built the capital, and beyond its walls are the cultivated lands. The whole settlement is surrounded by hills with temples.

From the wall of the acropolis the country is divided into 12 sectors by 12 radial lines. The inhabitants of each sector are called a tribe, and they and their lands are placed under the protection of one of the 12 gods, the dedication to be decided by lottery. Each citizen has an equal share, in the cultivated lands, in the city accommodation and in the wealth and goods of the state, and great care is taken to see that equality is preserved from generation to generation. This is achieved by the application of a mathematical code, based on the number 5040, to every detail of the community's structure and possessions. Even domestic equipment must be of standard size. In this respect Plato's law accords with that of the Peruvian Incas, who carried out regular inspections of dwelling-houses to ensure that even the cooking vessels were of the standard size and number.

Magnesia's ruling council consists of 360 members, divided into 12 groups who are on duty successively over the 12 months of each year. They are also divided by a caste system into four groups of ninety, and further complicated arrangements are laid down for their election. There are 60 local magistrates, five from each tribe, who each select 12 young retainers. Their duties include keeping the peace, defending the realm and maintaining public works. In bands of 60 they are stationed for one month in each of the 12 sectors in turn, and at the end of a year they repeat the same passage through the 12 tribes in reverse order. This, says Plato, gives them knowledge of every part of their native land in different seasons.

This image of a progress by monthly stages round a circle and back again is also that of the initiate's passage through 12 ordeals and the 12-episode careers of Gilgamesh and other such heroes. Astrologically, it is a journey through the zodiac; but that is not the limit of its reference. Ernest McClain, author of *The Pythagorean Plato*, sees Plato's numerical structures as a musical treatise. The careful enumeration of every detail in Magnesia is interpreted as a canon of sacred music, and McClain illustrates the wheel of the settlement divided into 12 unequal segments to represent musical intervals in the octave 2520 : 5040.

This interpretation, which is supported by Plato's repeated insistence on the value of choirs and sacred music, prompts further inquiry into that hitherto-neglected aspect of traditional societies, the magic by which they were enchanted. No doubt it was largely generated by scientific manipulation of sounds. Orpheus ruled a harmonious kingdom by music alone, and the power of music was so well known to ancient rulers that they prohibited all modes but those which contributed to the enchantment of their realms. Plato himself said that forms of music precede and determine forms of government.

Plato's idea of 12-tribe communities, founded and maintained on ideal principles, was meant literally. The difficulty, of course, lay in finding unspoilt, adult citizens willing and worthy to inhabit it. Plato overcame the problem by depicting the perfect, mathematical order of society in imitation of the cosmos, and recommending to future community founders that they adopt it as their model and copy it as far as possible, always being ready to compromise between the ideal and the practical. The twelve tribes of Magnesia were to live in much the same way as the ancient Greeks had lived in their 12-tribe amphictyonies, but Plato was not merely copying old forms. Magnesia was drawn from the original model, from the same cosmological pattern which has been the ground plan of sacred societies from times beyond reckoning. In its most abstract form it is a codification of number; then it is a musical harmony, a synthesis of geometric types, a cosmological diagram; finally it comes to earth as a perfectly ordered, magically enchanted human society.

THE NEW JERUSALEM AND THE TWELVE TRIBES REUNITED

The birth of Christ approximately coincided with the start of the Piscean Age. Such periods traditionally bring vision and spiritual renewal, and the dawn of Pisces was a time of millennial expectations. Led by the esoteric scholars of the Essene monasteries, the Jews awaited the imminent fulfilment of prophecy and the return from captivity of the missing ten tribes of Israel, whose reunion with Judah and Benjamin at Jerusalem would precede the renewal of divine government on earth. The early Christians, who apparently drew much of their tradition from the Essenes, shared a similar hope.

St John on the island of Patmos described his vision of the celestial 12-tribe city, the New Jerusalem, 'coming down from God out of heaven, prepared as a bride adorned for her husband' (Revelation 21:2). Twelve angels stood by its 12 gates, which were placed in groups of three at the four quarters and were inscribed with the names of the 12 tribes of Israel. The 12 gates were also 12 pearls. There were 12 foundations to the city wall, each bearing one of the names of the 12 Apostles and garnished with one of 12 precious stones. The city was shaped as a cube measuring 12,000 furlongs on every side, and the measure of its wall was 144 cubits. In the centre was the Tree of Life which yielded 12 different kinds of fruit, one for every month in the year.

This image of an ideal, 12-gated city occurs long before Christianity in cosmologies and social patterns throughout the East. According to the New Testament scholar, A.S. Geyser, the Essenes of the Qumran monastery planned the new Temple with 12 gates, one for each of the tribes. Moreover, 'they organized their daily lives in a division of twelve; they planned their army and logistics for the eschatological battle against the forces of Belial on the basis of twelve tribes...'

It is likely that John the Baptist, Jesus's teacher and initiator, was of the Qumran order. After the Baptist's arrest (Matthew 4: 12-17), Jesus went to Capernaum in Galilee in fulfilment of Isaiah's prophecy; for that was the territory of Zebulon and Naphthali, and those two were the first of the ten tribes to be carried into captivity in 734 BC. It was therefore expected that they would be the first to make their return to the Holy Land. Geyser suggests that behind Jesus's mission, in succession to that of John the Baptist, was the idea of preparing the lost tribes of Israel for their destined reassembly at Jerusalem.

The 12 disciples were symbolic of the 12 tribes. In Matthew 10 is the account of how Jesus summoned his college of 12, gave them spiritual power over demons and diseases, and sent them out among 'the lost sheep of the house of Israel', avoiding both Gentiles and Samaritans. After the death of Jesus, his followers were led by his brother James whose New Testament epistle is addressed 'to the twelve tribes which are scattered abroad'.

In this link between early Christianity and the prophesied reconstitution of the 12-tribe Israelite amphictyony is a deep religious mystery. The Jews believe literally in the eventual regrouping of all twelve tribes of Israel, ten of which are still 'scattered among the nations of the world' and unidentified. Yet the symbolism behind this theme of return and renewal reaches beyond any one people or country. It signifies the rediscovery or revelation of a traditional world order, reflected in the constitutions of all the 12-tribe nations recorded by history. This order of society is constantly associated in legend with times of the highest culture and prosperity, as in the days of Solomon's 12-tribe kingdom. Whenever the ancient secret is lost and its doctrines forgotten, the initiate's quest is for their recovery. Thus Jesus appointed 12 disciples and St John revealed the traditional pattern of the ideal, 12-gated city, intending thereby to hasten the return of sacred order to earth and to prepare their generation for enlightened response to the dawning Age of Pisces.

THE GLOBAL AMPHICTYONY

The most intriguing aspect of these studies in 12-tribe nations is the former worldwide application of the 12-fold order. The image of a global amphictyony occurs in several passages of Plato, and it is implied by the ancient chorographies, the 12-nation charts of the earth described more fully in Chapter 11. It is difficult to say how relevant this image may be to present times, but it is certainly appealing; and it certainly appealed to the philosophers of ancient times, when it may even have been a reality.

The natural symbol of the earth, peacefully inhabited by a brotherhood of twelve nations, is the dodecahedron, the regular 12-sided shape whose faces are made up of 12 pentagons. The pentagon in the symbolism of geometry represents humanity. Plato in the *Timaeus* classified the dodecahedron as the fifth and last of the regular solid figures, encompassing all the others. It represents the ether, and mystics have claimed that the essential form of the earth's subtle body is the dodecahedron. This figure is also the perfect model for 12-tribe nations, for it is a curious fact of geometry that 12 equal spheres will fit exactly round a central thirteenth, each touching the central sphere and four of its neighbours.

The image of the earth in its ideal, 12-sided form was accepted by Plato, and this is significant because Plato was above all a revivalist, and he described ancient institutions as an incentive to their renewal. In *Critias* (113) he tells how, in the beginning, the 12 gods divided the world up between them, each taking an equal portion as their special province. In *Phaedo* (110) he describes the world as seen from above, from beyond the grossness of the atmosphere, as a glorious dodecahedron. It looks like 'one of those balls which are covered with twelve pieces of leather, with patches of various colours'. It is the same world as we inhabit, but far more pure and beautiful. The colours we know are but dull reflections of the sparkling colours of that world. Flowers, trees, animals, lakes, mountains and precious stones are more perfect than here; the climate is always benevolent, there are no diseases and people live happily to great ages, possessed of keener senses and more wisdom than we enjoy and in direct communication with the gods.

This picture of the paradisial earth, garnished with different kinds of precious stones on its 12 sides, is reminiscent of St John's celestial city, the New Jerusalem. Similar types of images are universal in mythology and constitute one of its most attractive mysteries. The idea of our mundane world, transformed into a place of ideal beauty and splendour, is an apparent fantasy; yet mystics in all ages have glimpsed it, have been convinced of its reality and have located it on a plane not far removed from the level of normal, modern perception. The Irish poet, who in 1918 wrote *The Candle of Vision* under the name A.E., described a vision of the multi-coloured plane, through which, he said, 'I knew that the Golden Age was all about me, and it was we who had been blind to it but that it had never passed away from the world.' Mythological descriptions of paradise bear the same implication, that Elysium, Agartha and the Isles of the Blessed are not entirely removed from our earthly existence, for these ideal kingdoms have at one time been established here below, are still accessible to those who seek them and will one day be restored to common perception.

Here again we are confronted with the mystery which haunts every inquiry into the system of zodiacal societies and landscapes, the mystery of their reputed origin through revelation. The recurring vision, which inspires people at different times to reshape their whole countries on a formal, cosmological, 12-fold pattern, must indeed be compelling. Its full significance can hardly be grasped without experiencing it, but its general form is clear from Plato's, St John's and other seers' accounts of it. We hear of a radiant earth or city, perfectly proportioned, sparkling with 12 coloured jewels. It is the archetypal model for the most perfect, attainable state of affairs on earth, where the 12 different races, each protected by one of the 12 gods and praising him in the mode of music which is appropriate to his character, form a global amphictyony, thus restoring the earth to her natural and pristine state of harmony with the heavens.

THE NUMERICAL CREATION

Numbers were not invented but discovered. They existed as unmanifest archetypes before there was anything for them to quantify. When there were no three objects, nor four or five of anything, the numbers 3, 4 and 5 were already immanent, and when creation took place, they were available to give it form and proportion. This perception gave rise to the creation myth behind ancient philosophy, that the Creator's originating thought was of a perfectly harmonious code of number, and from that pattern developed all the forces and phenomena of nature.

The foundation formula which produced 12-tribe, astrologically arranged nations was a numerical imitation of the Creator's thought. It was a codification of the geometric proportions and musical harmonies which underlie nature's forms and patterns of motion. The priests of ancient Egypt, says Plato in the *Laws*, upheld this code for over ten thousand years as their ultimate source of law. All craftsmen and artists, particularly musicians who have the greatest influence on the forms of society, were required to compose their works in accordance with those harmonies and proportions which were specified in the code. Innovations and uncanonical harmonies were forbidden. The result was that the same high standards of art and civilization were maintained in all ages.

The greatest of all the works of art, produced by the cosmic canon of proportion, was the state constitution. From the ground plans of Plato's Magnesia, the New Jerusalem of Revelation and 25 other sources is obtained the diagram shown in figure 25, which

82

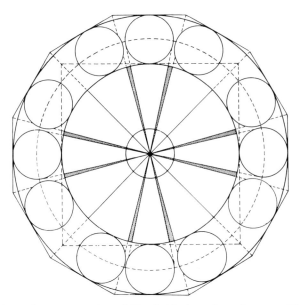

Fig. 25. A schematic reconstruction of Plato's ideal, twelve-tribe state. The dark sectors represent the common ground for roads or paths between tribal boundaries. The two inner circles represent the city with the acropolis at the centre, surrounded by the cultivated land. Around the outside are hills with temples. This figure is an image of the canon of harmonies and proportions which set the pattern for all twelve-tribe societies.

is a geometric image of the traditional cosmology. It symbolizes complete orders of natural phenomena on many different levels. From it are generated all the standard types of geometry, measure and music; it depicts the order of the heavens, reconciles the ever-moving circle of eternity with the fixed and rational square of earth, and provided the ground plan and social model for the nations of the 12 tribes.

The basic figure in this diagram is the 'squared circle', symbol of harmonious union between heaven and earth, spirit and matter, nature and civilization. It is made up of the square which encloses the circle representing the earth, and the circle which passes through the centres of the 12 small circles. The measure round the perimeter of the square is the same as the circumference of the circle.

The 12 small circles, placed tangent to the earth circle in four groups to represent the four seasons and directions, are the 12 moons or months in the year, the 12 astrological ages, zodiacal signs, gods, tribes and notes in the chromatic scale of music. In the dimensions of this diagram, the radius of each of these lunar circles is 2160, referring to the 2160 miles in the moon's diameter and the 2160 years in one astrological month. The circle around which they stand has a diameter of 7920, which is the number of miles in the mean diameter of the earth. This illuminates a most striking fact of astronomy, that the earth and moon together construct the squared circle – the square and circle of equal perimeters. Moreover, the figure that emerges is not proportioned by meaningless or arbitrary numbers, but represents that codification of number which was the essence of the ancient canon of harmonies.

THE TWELVE AND THE SEVEN

Creation proceeds from unity to diversity, and the fount and origin of all numbers is likewise unity or the number one. It is unique among numbers in that it is not generated by any of the others, either by addition or multiplication, but itself generates all of them. Every number is produced by the addition of a series of ones, and the reproductive power of the Monad is demonstrated below, where the squaring of a series of the numbers made up of the number one produces all the nine base numbers, both forwards and backwards.

$$
\begin{array}{rcr}
1 \times 1 & = & 1 \\
11 \times 11 & = & 121 \\
111 \times 111 & = & 12321 \\
1111 \times 1111 & = & 1234321 \\
11111 \times 11111 & = & 123454321 \\
111111 \times 111111 & = & 12345654321 \\
1111111 \times 1111111 & = & 1234567654321 \\
11111111 \times 11111111 & = & 123456787654321 \\
111111111 \times 111111111 & = & 12345678987654321 \\
\end{array}
$$

Being indivisible, the number one is the natural symbol of any integral whole and is therefore used to represent the cosmos or universal system regarded as one organism.

The apparent predominance of the number ten within the field of number is only superficial, for the number appointed by nature as the framework of arithmetic is the number twelve. As the number of order, it is associated with authority and the sun, and its symbolic opposite, representing the free spirit of nature, is the number seven. These two numbers have a peculiar, hidden relationship, and their distinctive arithmetical and musical functions have made them important symbols in the philosophy of number. An eloquent tribute to the powers of the numbers twelve and seven was composed by Fabre d'Olivet, of which the following parts are extracted from his book *Music Explained as Science and Art*, translated by Joscelyn Godwin.

The number 12, formed from the ternary and the quaternary, is the symbol of the Universe and the measure of tone. In expressing myself thus, I speak simply as the interpreter of the ancient philosophers and the modern theosophers, and say openly what the hierophant of Eleusis and of Thebes confided only to initiates in the secrecy of the sanctuary. What is more, it is by no means merely an opinion maintained by a single people, at a certain time, in a particular country of the earth; it is a scientific and sacred dogma accepted among all nations from the north of Europe to the most eastern parts of Asia. Pythagoras, Timaeus of Locris, Plato, in giving the dodecahedron as symbol for the Universe, were expounding the ideas of the Egyptians, the Chaldaeans, and the Greeks. These peoples had long since attributed the government of Nature to twelve principal gods. The Persians followed in this regard the doctrine of the Chaldaeans, and the Romans adopted that of the Greeks. Even at the extremities of Europe, the Scandinavians, in admitting the duodecimal division, also counted twelve rulers of the Universe whom they named the Aser...

After the number 12, product of the multiplication of 3 and 4, the most generally revered number was the number 7, formed from the sum of 3 and 4. It was considered in the sanctuaries of Thebes and Eleusis as the symbol of the Soul of the World unfolding itself in the bosom of the Universe and giving life to it. Macrobius, who has transmitted many ancient mysteries to us, tells that this soul, distributed among the seven spheres of the world which it moves and animates and from which it produces the harmonic tones, was designated emblematically by the number 7, or figuratively by the seven-holed flute placed in the hands of Pan, the God of the Universe...

The number 7 was called by the Pythagoreans the Eternal Virgin, the reason being that it is the only number within the first ten which neither breeds nor is generated. In other words, it is not generated as, for example, 6 is generated as the product of 3×2, nor does it give birth, as do 2 and 4 in producing 8, 2 and 5 in

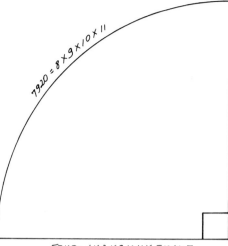

Fig. 26. The foundation figure of cosmological geometry is a circle which expresses in its dimensions the first twelve numbers. The numbers 1-7, multiplied together, form the radius, and numbers 8-11 measure the quadrant. The whole scheme, exemplified by Plato's city, the New Jerusalem and other such traditional world-images, is framed in units of the number 12.

producing 10, and so on. Only that which has not been born can be called eternal. Thus the number 7 was applied to Athena, who came from no womb, but sprung fully armed from the head of Zeus. The design of her temple on the Acropolis contained many symbolic references to the number 7, and her esoteric number, calculated by adding the numerical values of the letters in her name is 77.

Another function of the number 7 within the first ten numbers is to provide the point of balance. The numbers on either side of 7 are arranged symmetrically:

$$1 \times 2 \times 3 \times 4 \times 5 \times 6 = 720$$
$$8 \times 9 \times 10 = 720$$

When 720 is multiplied by the missing 7, the product is 5040. This is the number which Plato emphasizes and which has special prominence in the dimensions of the cosmological diagram (figure 25) from which Plato and St John derived their images of ideal cities.

This diagram is entirely framed by the number 12, as is appropriate for a symbol of the universal structure. But at its heart is enfolded the spiritual number 7. The primary figure in the diagram is the circle with its circumference passing through the centres of the 12 lunar circles. The radius of that circle is the sum of the earth's radius and the moon's radius, or 3960 + 1080 = 5040 miles. The quadrant of its circumference is 7920 miles. In those

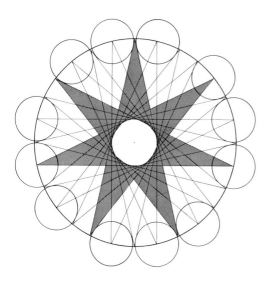

Fig. 27. The framework of the 12-tribe diagram neatly accommodates the 28 points of the lunar cycle, as well as the 7-pointed figure (shaded).

dimensions are encoded all the numbers from 1 to 11, and the number which frames them all is 12.

$$1 \times 2 \times 3 \times 4 \times 5 \times 6 \times 7 = 5040 = \text{circle's radius}$$
$$8 \times 9 \times 10 \times 11 = 7920 = \text{circle's quadrant}$$

As the product of the first 7 numbers multiplied together, 5040 is a symbol of the number 7. The 12-tribe diagram also includes the geometry of 7, reconciling it with the duodecimal framework. This is shown in figure 27, where a regular 28-pointed figure is seen to fit neatly within the 12-fold frame. The 28 points represent the 4×7 or 28 phases of the moon during the lunar month, and so the diagram serves as a calendar of lunar as well as solar cycles.   *27*

The development of the cosmological diagram parallels the most crucial development in human history, the decline of the primordial, wandering life and the foundation of civilizations. The original circle, with its radius of 5040 or 7 units, represents the natural, nomadic state of existence, when the dominant numerical symbol was the Septenary. The 7 stars ruled over a sacred landscape with 7 hills and 7 springs, and the 7 notes of Pan's pipe made the simple, natural scale of rustic music.

With the coming of civilization, the pattern of archaic life under the reign of 7-fold spirit is overlaid by a more formal cosmology. The square, representing settlement, is added to the circle to form the squared circle symbol, and the diagram is completed by the 12 outer circles of moons, months and tribes. With this development, the primordial sacred landscape of the 7 wandering gods is apportioned between the 12 settled gods of the zodiac and the 12 settled tribes beneath them. To the 7 notes of the shepherd's pipe are added five more, making the 12-note, chromatic scale of civilized music.

In thus developing the foundation plan of the 12-tribe societies, we acquire insight into that deepest of mysteries, the origin of civilizations. Legends tell of Apollo and other culture-bearing, solar heroes, who killed the earth serpent and placed an organized priesthood in charge of the ancient oracles and spirit shrines. These legends, and the birth of civilization which they allegorize, are often seen as triumphs of the male over the female, the artificial over the natural, reason and materialism over imagination and the spirit. They can indeed bear that interpretation, but so also can be interpreted the development of civilization. Most of us appreciate the comforts of civilization, and we do not therefore clamour for its abolition, even though repression and injustice are common to all its forms. The ideal, as exhibited in the cosmological diagram, is a settled, ordered society, based on human nature and spirit as symbolized by the number 7, and attuned to the orderly cycles of the heavens by the number 12.

In this diagram we do not see the victory of the solar element over the lunar, but a harmonious union, the sacred marriage between two elements as sought by the philosophical alchemists. As a social model, it reconciles the two conflicting urges in human nature, as represented in the Old Testament by Abel, the nomadic herdsman, and Cain, the settled agriculturist – the cowboy and the farmer, the dreamer and the legislator. Plato promised that its restoration would bring the greatest possible amount of happiness to the largest possible number of people. Made effective by the arts of priestcraft, it served as a Grail to the societies that adopted it, creating in them a state of mind which we compare to an enchantment.

This brings us to the nub of our subject: the nature of those priestly arts which created and maintained the enchantment of whole countries and nations.

7

The science
of enchanting landscapes

The creation of sacred landscapes and 12-tribe societies, attuned
to the rhythms of nature, was a magical work of priestcraft. All
branches of art and science were brought together in one system
under the guiding standard of that cosmological formula, geometrically represented in figure 25. Plato referred to it in the *Republic*
as the 'pattern in the heavens' which provides the ideal foundation
plan either for a political state or for the individual world-view.

A question which puzzled Plato was how the traditional cosmology was first codified and how it came into the possession of
the first lawgivers. At the very beginning of the *Laws* he discusses
the legendary origins of ancient states such as Crete and Sparta.
In every case, he finds, their laws are said to have been given to
them in the first place by a god, by Zeus to the Cretans and Apollo
to the Spartans. The laws were dictated to certain wise men in the
way that Jehovah gave the commandments to Moses. Referring to
the Egyptian canon of sacred music, which was to provide the
enchantment in his own ideal state, Plato said that it must have
been the work of a god or god-like individual, and that the
Egyptians themselves attributed it to Isis.

The traditional history of 12-tribe states is that in the beginning
the gods themselves ruled on earth. They apportioned the world
between themselves into 12 allotments, and similarly divided each
country, giving to each god his area of influence. In those days,
the wandering tribes passed through all twelve signs of the zodiac
in the course of their annual circuit of their sacred centre. The
gods moved among them, instructing them by oracles and appearing
in person at their festivals. Science, religion and legislation were
therefore unnecessary, nor was there any need to develop arts and
crafts, everything being provided by nature and divine revelation.

The departure of the gods and the beginning of settlement and
agriculture are coeval events. As a substitute for their direct

guidance, the gods confide to the keeping of the wisest men a code of law which, if instituted and upheld, will reproduce virtually the same conditions as when the gods ruled directly. Under this law the people are divided into 12 tribes which are settled in zodiacal order in the country around the central sanctuary. Other aspects of the law regulated music, lore and customs, the times and places of festivals and all other matters, from state ritual to details of domestic life. Such communities, fashioned entirely by one law, are literally held under enchantment.

There is no doubt that such a law existed, and that it constituted the primordial tradition at the origin of civilized culture. The means by which it came into human possession are quite unknown but, once established, the divine law was faithfully upheld by a succession of initiated priests.

The first requirement of a ruling priesthood is to locate and occupy the naturally powerful centres of spiritual energy in the landscape. This involves the use of geomancy, meaning divination through the earth or earth magic. Through geomancy are discovered the most effective sites and designs for temples in relation to the spiritual energy field of the country as a whole. The many sciences which contribute to geomancy include astronomy and geology, for temples should be sited at natural meeting-places between the powers of heaven and earth. This principle is now recognized by archaeologists, who have discovered in recent years that temples and old stone monuments in all countries are related to their surroundings in two ways, astronomically and geologically. The stone circles of Britain and the stone wheels of the North American Indians, the megalithic chambered mounds in Ireland and Europe, the temples of Mexico, Peru, Greece, Egypt and the East; all these are found to have been orientated to the heavenly bodies. At certain moments of the year they were illuminated by sun, moon or starlight, and in that form the heavenly gods entered their temples, contributing their powers to the magical rites performed there.

Megalithic monuments and the more elaborate temples which succeeded them are also found to have been sited in connection with the earthly powers. They are generally situated above or near geological fault lines, over subterranean springs and watercourses, at nodal points in the earth's energy field. These places are centres of geomagnetic and other measurable energies, but they are also vitalized by a more subtle force, traditionally identified with the spirits of the country and the souls of the dead.

Prehistoric mounds are reputed to be haunted by ghosts of the old people buried there, and mysterious lights and flames are seen playing over them. These lights and phantoms, says Paul Devereux in his book *Earth Lights*, are manifestations of earth energy which occur at places where the underlying rocks are under pressure, as is the case in fissures and fault lines. To the ancients they indicated places of power, where spirit flows strongly and where magical rites can most effectively be performed. Such places have a natural function as sites for necromancy and oracles, for communications with the dead and the daemons of earth. Through their position on the earth's sensitive places, where the veins and currents of terrestrial energy are centred, ancient temples were adapted as places of spiritual invocation, and also as amplifiers. A legend of the temple at Jerusalem says that it was the centre of a network of underground water channels, which spread outwards to all parts of the country. Through the medium of this vascular system everything done in the temple was amplified and broadcast. The influence of chants and ritual permeated through the veins and energy field of the earth to wide and general effect. Temples and ritual sites were centres of rule, where laws were proclaimed and the ideal of a cosmically ordered society was symbolically reproduced. Order was thus maintained, partly by example and the emphasizing of established custom, and partly by the magical qualities of the site itself. An example of such a site, described in Chapter 3, is that of the Althing, the Icelandic ritual assembly, which met at the most naturally powerful spot on the island, above the deepest fissure on its major fault line.

In the legend of the Jerusalem Temple, the light and energy which issued from the inner sanctum conveyed health, fertility and blessings. When the Temple was destroyed a spell was broken. Thus we conclude that the overall purpose of the ancient religious and magical science was to spread an enchantment over the twelve tribes of a nation, creating the atmosphere of a golden age.

Besides cosmology, geomancy, astronomy and astrology, the most important of the sciences which contributed to the enchantment was music. An enchantment, as its name implies, is created by chanting. Plato made the same play on words in stating that songs (*odai*) are charms (*epiodai*). In Book 2 of his *Laws* he says that the enchantment of his ideal city will be created by sacred music, derived from the cosmological canon of harmonies which Plato knew from his studies in Egypt. All the inhabitants of the city, men, women, children and servants, must join chorus groups and practise the correct songs and dances. There are three types of chorus, for children, for people up to thirty, and for those between thirty and sixty. Older citizens, who are past singing and dancing, must recite the same legends as provide the themes for the songs. The music, the dances and the stories are all to be composed from ideal models so as to create the best possible form of enchantment.

To maintain the enchantment, says Plato, the people must continually hear and repeat the traditional songs, charms and stories, but in constantly changing forms. The themes and musical modes remain the same, but their expressions ever vary. This implies an epic narrative, accompanied by a ceaseless chant which reflects the various episodes of the story, and reflects also the progression of seasons and astrological cycles.

We are led to conclude that, at the beginning of every sacred society or amphictyonic league, the lawgiving priests created a musical reformation, adapting the local melodies and folk songs to a 12-part chant, reflecting the harmonies of heaven. One of the 12 notes in the musical scale was allotted to each of the tribes according to their zodiacal signs. The music of each tribe was keyed to that particular note, was heard at all the festivals within their territory and set the tone of the sacred music in their temples. By a round of festivals and chanted liturgies in each of the 12 tribal territories in turn, a perpetual chant was maintained throughout the year, and at annual meetings in the national 28 sanctuary, 12 choirs came together to imitate with their voices the full harmony of the heavenly spheres.

Many composers, both ancient and modern, have created musical zodiacs, placing the 12 notes in the scale under the 12 zodiacal signs and thus attempting to represent the music of the spheres. 29 The oldest surviving tone-zodiac, in Ptolemy's *Harmonics*, equates the Greek two-octave scale with the 12 signs. Modern compositions have generally been based on the single-octave, equally tempered chromatic scale. The most interesting of these tone-zodiacs are described in Joscelyn Godwin's *Harmonies of Heaven and Earth*, where the principles behind them are fully discussed from both

Fig. 28. The 12 angels, each with a different musical instrument, carved on the minstrels' gallery at Exeter Cathedral, recall the days when a twelve-part Gregorian chant upheld a religious enchantment over tribes and countries. In China the 12 semi-tones in the scale corresponded to certain lengths of pipe, each with its own pitch, which served also as standard units of measure.

musical and astrological points of view. One of the examples he illustrates, by the Irish musicologist, Michael McMullin, is reproduced in figure 30. Other tone-zodiacs are arranged differently, and it was no doubt the case that the interpretations of celestial music, given to astrologically ordered societies, varied from one to the other. There is even a hint, implied in the 12-nation unions of ancient sacred geography, of a conceptual global choir, celebrating the full range of celestial music in all its modes and aspects.

As music was codified and correlated with the 12-sign zodiac, so also was myth. The various 12-part epic myths, from King Arthur to Gilgamesh, are known to incorporate figures and episodes from earlier mythologies of the stars and planets. It is apparent that the lawgivers refashioned local legends, weaving them into a 12-part heroic cycle which moved the drama through each of the 12 zodiacal territories in the course of the year. In virgin country, as in tenth-century Iceland where there was no existing folklore, ancient sagas were adapted to the landscape, one division subdivided into three being given to each quarter of the island. These

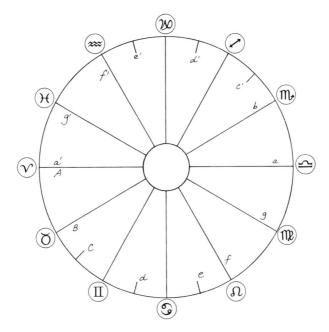

Fig. 29. Ptolemy's tone-zodiac.

reflected the character of the region, referred to the names and genealogies of the families who settled there, and named mountains and landscape features according to the mythic events which were attached to them. Thus in early generations was created from wilderness a mythological landscape.

Our overall picture of a zodiacal landscape is of a countryside enchanted by sacred art. The geomantic, astronomical, musical and other techniques which comprised that art were subordinate to a numerical code of cosmology, representing the harmonic structure of the universe. That pattern, in the form of a 12-sign zodiacal circle, was imprinted on landscapes around the sacred mountain sanctuary of the nation. Laws and customs were established and made traditional. Every aspect of life was governed by the same set of standards, and uniformity was imposed down to the last domestic detail. Songs and sagas passed unchanged through each generation. Feasts and ceremonies were held throughout the year, always on the same day and at the same place. Everything possible was done to avert the threat of innovation. Even in decadent times, when the guiding principles behind the wisdom of

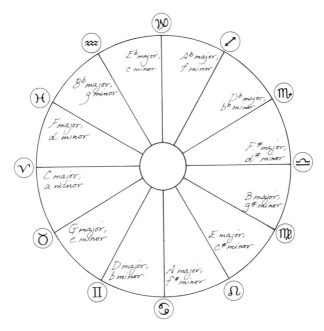

Fig. 30. The tone-zodiac proposed by Michael McMullin.

the state founders had become neglected, the enchantment was maintained for a time by blind adherence to custom.

Echoes of a former enchantment linger in many parts of the world. In remote countries of the East, where the temple chant is even now maintained, travellers speak of entering a different reality, where spirits still occupy their country shrines and minor miracles are everyday occurrences. The spell of music can survive extreme poverty and oppression. In Haiti, for example, the peaceful atmosphere which prevails even in the most destitute quarters of town is sometimes credited to the splendid Gregorian, African-accented chant which is sung in the cathedral and contributes to the local tone and mood. In various countries evidence is found of a former nationwide canon of music, effective on every level, in the resemblance between the ecclesiastical chant and the folk music of the provinces. When Cecil Sharp and Sabine Baring-Gould were collecting surviving English country songs during the 1880s, they were surprised to find that their tunes, though often fitted to coarse ballads, were based on the classical modes of music. As Cecil Sharp wrote:

English folk-tunes are cast in the Dorian, Phrygian, Mixolydian, Aeolian and Ionian (major) modes... The majority of our English folk-tunes, say two-thirds, are in the major or Ionian mode. The remaining third is fairly evenly divided between the Mixolydian, Dorian and Aeolian modes.

These old tunes were clearly the work of educated composers, probably monastic, and had been instituted through the bardic fraternity to the benefit of rural culture.

The power of sacred chant over countrysides and people is illustrated in the history of medieval monasticism. Cistercian monks from the beginning of the twelfth century retired to the loneliest, most barren districts of Europe, as had the Celtic saints before them, and lived in the utmost simplicity, spending every possible moment in prayer and chanting. With a few years the influence of their chant changed the entire character of their surroundings. The former wildernesses grew rich and populous, crafts and husbandry flourished and people generally, though inevitably prone to normal human suffering, were content and high-spirited. The monks themselves contributed nothing practical to the management and working of their great estates. They merely chanted, and the angelic harmonies they uttered produced a corresponding order in the country around them.

PART II

8

Zodiacal wheels on ancient landscapes

The most imaginative and far-reaching works on the sacred geography of Greece, Italy and the eastern Mediterranean are those of the French scholar, Jean Richer. He is the distinguished author of books on Gérard de Nerval, Rimbaud, Shakespeare and other writers in the esoteric tradition, and his studies of symbolism in literature, particularly in Nerval, led him to investigate that tradition at its roots, in the relics and records of antiquity.

During the 1950s Richer became interested in features of Greek temples, incuding their siting and orientations. Many of these present anomalies which have long puzzled archaeologists. The axis of a temple was generally aligned upon the rising point of one of the heavenly bodies, symbolizing the god to whom it was dedicated, but not all orientations can be explained in that way. In his book of 1962, *The Earth, the Temple and the Gods*, Vincent Scully showed that temple sites and plans were often related to natural features in the landscape, to hills and mountains whose shapes were emblematic of certain deities. Richer developed another thesis: that the orientations, sculptured designs and other symbolic features of Greek temples were of astrological significance, indicating the meaning of each temple within a zodiacal pattern which extended over an entire country. This was evidenced in his book of 1967, *Géographie sacrée du monde grec*, which received an award from the Académie française and was followed in 1985 by *Géographie sacrée dans le monde romain*.

In the first book Richer described four major zodiac wheels across large tracts of Greece and Asia Minor, with centres at Delphi, Athens, the island of Delos and Sardis in Anatolia. The axes defining the twelve zodiacal divisions were marked by temples and famous mountain peaks, and in each sector Richer found references on many different levels to its ruling astrological sign.

The evidence was from coins, vases, inscriptions, temple pediments and orientations, sculptures, place names, local myths and legends, religious traditions and ancient texts. Delphi and Delos are known to have been centres of 12-tribe amphictyonies, so the idea of astrological landscapes around them is historically justified; but the zodiacal circles and their dividing lines which Richer identified were far more extensive and deeply ingrained than anyone had previously imagined.

Richer's book of 1970, *Delphes, Délos et Cumes*, gives a remarkable account of the events which led up to his discoveries. They were preceded by a series of dreams. One of the dreams, which Richer describes as oracular, came when he was living in Athens near the Parthenon, high on the western slope of Lycabettos, the pyramid-shaped mount associated with Gaea. The dream seemed to visit him in response to a question which had been on his mind: why was a sanctuary to Athena Pronaia sited at the entrance to Delphi so that travellers from Athens could not avoid seeing it? Richer dreamed that he was looking at a *kouros* statue from behind. Slowly the figure turned in a clockwise direction to face him. It was similar to two *kouroi* in the National Museum at Athens, figures of an ideally proportioned youth representing Apollo, god of light.

It seemed to Richer that the dream was hinting at some kind of link between Delphi, the great Apollo sanctuary, and Athens, where the dream occurred and where Apollo and Athena both had temples. Following the dream came his first important discovery.

Still half asleep, I took the first map of Greece which came to hand – it was the little map at the end of the *Guide Bleu* – and traced out the line between Delphi and Athens. To my amazement, when the line was extended it went on to Delos and to Camiros in Rhodes, site of the oldest sanctuary of Apollo on the island...

Delos is the legendary birthplace of both Apollo and Artemis. The antiquity of Delphi as the Greek omphalos, navel or world centre is indicated in the old legend that when Zeus released two eagles from the two ends of the earth, Delphi was the place where they met.

In the course of several years Richer found other lines of sanctuaries passing through Delphi. A line from Tempe due north corresponds with the route by which, according to Pausanias, the

Fig. 31. Mount Parnassus above Delphi has the characteristic shape of a national sacred mountain.

cult of Apollo had reached Delphi. An alignment of sacred mountains, from Parnassus at Delphi through the Acro-Corinth above the Corinthian temple of Apollo to the Cretan Mount Ida, recalls verses in the Homeric Hymn to Apollo which say that the Delphic priesthood was originally from Minoan Crete. Sardis in Asia Minor is on the same latitude as Delphi, due east, and the lines from Delphi to Sardis and Mount Ida form an angle of 60° or two 30° sectors of a circle. A pattern began to emerge, and Richer saw it as a great astrological wheel with its hub at the oracle site of Delphi.

Numerous and diverse clues enabled Richer to complete the Delphi zodiac and to identify the signs appropriate to its various sectors. To the west and a few degrees north of Delphi is Leukas, a name meaning light, the traditional site of the death and rebirth of the sun god and the scene of ritual sacrifices to Apollo. According to Strabo, the people there celebrated Apollo's spring feast day by attaching feathers and a flock of birds to a condemned criminal and pushing him off a high cliff into the sea. Richer took Leukas to represent spring and therefore Aries, the spring equinoctial sign

99

for about 2000 years up to the time of Christ. He placed the line due west from Delphi under Aries, and its extension due east towards Sardis under the opposing sign, Libra. When the other signs are added in clockwise order, Richer's original line through Delphi, Athens and Delos is found to be a Virgo-Pisces axis. Each of the six paired lines of the zodiac represent a pair of signs, and Richer's evidence is that these influenced the forms and symbols of the regions they bordered. Apart from its own astrological emblems, the art of each sector also refers to the dominant symbol of the quarter in which it stands. These four symbols also represent the four seasons of the year, the panther for summer, a lion or pride of lions killing a bull for spring, lions killing a deer for summer, and the autumnal serpent.

As Richer spread his lines across the Aegean Sea, the Mediterranean and the lands bordering them, he detected symmetries on an even larger scale. The pattern of sites was sometimes indicated by temple orientations. Apollo's temple at Delos faces west, a strange anomaly since most Apollo temples look eastward. Richer discovered that its axis points to Hermione, which stands on the Delphi-to-Mount-Ida line where it strikes the coast of mainland Greece. He suspected that Hermione must have been an important cult centre of Apollo, and from Pausanias he learnt that there had once been three Apollonian temples there, as well as an earlier temple to Helios. Due east from Delos, at the same distance as Hermione and on the same latitude, is the third aligned temple of Apollo, at Didyma on the Anatolian coast, a former oracle centre below Mount Mykale. This line forms the Aries-Libra axis of Richer's Delian zodiac.

Another unusual orientation is that of Apollo's temple at Bassae, which has its entrance to the north-north-east. Scully thought that the architects meant to indicate the flat-topped Mount Ithome, sacred to Zeus, but the temple is not directly orientated on the mountain. Richer discovered that its axis is aligned precisely towards the centre of its zodiacal sector, the omphalos at Delphi.

Images on coins and figures carved on temples were Richer's two main sources of astrological symbolism. The use of coins is supposed to have been introduced into Greece in the seventh century BC. It came from Lydia, whose capital, Sardis, was one of the zodiac centres, and the earliest coins were stamped with zodiacal signs. Up to the end of the fifth century all coin designs

Fig. 32. Forming the main axis of Greek sacred geography is the straight line between the principal Apollonian oracle centres.

A Kerkyras (Corfu).   C Athens.   E Delos.
B Delphi (Mount Parnassus).   D Prasaias.   F Lindos, Rhodes.

were either zodiacal or represented deities. Many of the zodiacal figures were in the Egyptian, Babylonian or Celtic tradition. Richer found numerous references on the coinage of different cities to the astrological sectors in which they were located.

He also found that the figures and groups carved on temple pediments were not chosen at random, but were designed to illustrate the character of each temple and its site, with allusions to its position within the countrywide astrological scheme. One example he describes is the temple of Apollo at Delphi. Its place at the heart of the Delphi zodiac is expressed in its symbolism, beginning with its orientation. It faces the midsummer sunrise, and in the other direction its axis points to sunset at midwinter. Its two pediments, front and back, had at their corners the symbolic beasts of the four seasons and quarters. The north-east pediment, towards the midsummer sun, shows Apollo with three maidens (spring) and three youths (summer). On the south-west pediment

35

101

Zeus, the ruler of winter, stands at the centre with Hera, and is flanked by two groups of deities symbolic of winter and autumn. Groups of zodiacal gods are in battle with the giants of winter.

Statues of the old gods stood in their temples, and there are several references by Greek authors to their occasional animation. Made of natural materials, wood, stone, ivory or earthenware, they were charged through priestly rituals with sacred energy, and gave oracular counsel. The gods were also represented on a larger scale in temple precincts and high places about the countryside in *33* the form of colossal statues. The most famous colossus, near or perhaps astride the harbour at Rhodes, represented Helios, the sun god. Before its collapse in an earthquake in 224 BC it stood 70 cubits or up to 120 feet tall; its maker, Chares of Lindos, specialized in colossal statues. So also did Pheidias in the fifth century BC. His first work, an enthroned Zeus made of ivory with a cloak of gold, was commissioned by the Elians. Among his other colossi were the Apollo of Calamis, the Zeus and Hercules at Lysippus, the *34* Zeus at Olympia and a huge bronze Athena in the Acropolis at Athens, visible from far out at sea. Nor was this practice of erecting enormous statues confined to Grecian lands. In the French Auvergne a temple of Mercury stood near the summit of the Puy de Dôme, and above it, on the highest peak, was a gigantic statue of the Celtic Hermes.

In *Delphes, Délos et Cumes* Richer suggests that 12 colossal statues marked each of the 12 sectors of a zodiac. Charged with the same divine energy as the temple statues, they symbolized the astrological meaning of their regions and served as their magical guardians. His examples include the colossal figures of Castor and Pollux at Cape Sounion, representing Gemini in that sector of the Athens zodiac, and the Scorpio symbol, Pluto or Hades, which stood in effigy at Sinope, under Scorpio in the zodiac centered on Sardis. Another zodiacal figure, the carved lion on the island of Kea, is thought by Richer to be older than any of the other colossi and to have been part of an archaic astrological pattern which preceded the Delphic and other zodiac wheels. It has features in common with the Egyptian Sphinx, symbolizing the equinox.

The formal design of zodiacal landscapes around oracle centres is dated by Richer to about 2000 BC, when the Age of Taurus was giving way to Aries. First came the simple division of countries into four parts, corresponding to the four seasons. Later, between

Fig. 33. The colossus at Rhodes, a figure of the sun god, was erected in 279 BC and stood for 56 years until an earthquake toppled it. Colossal statues were known in antiquity throughout Greece and beyond. They are thought to have had astrological significance, denoting the god who reigned over the territory where each was placed.

Fig. 34. A reconstruction of the colossal Athena which stood in the Acropolis.

about 1000 and 800 BC, the twelve-part zodiac wheels were completed under Cretan and Phoenician influence. The system reached its fullest development around 600 BC. Its origins go back to very early times. Before the precession of the equinoxes had been measured, astronomers used a fixed sidereal zodiac, based on the distances between first magnitude stars whose heliacal risings marked the seasons of the year. The pattern of the heavens was reflected upon earth, each region being under a certain constellation. These relationships were permanent, and when the zodiac wheels were imprinted on the landscape, the ancient stellar symbolism of its various parts was preserved. Thus the usual symbols for the astrological signs and the quarters are amplified in each region by many others of archaic origin. The hare, for example, is an alternative symbol for Taurus, because its constellation, Lepus, stands close to Taurus in the sky. In the same way, the dolphin represents Capricorn, Pegasus is Aquarius and so on. Other images, mythologically associated with the zodiacal signs, are sometimes used as their symbols: the octopus or spiral for Cancer, the ear of corn for Virgo and the cup or amphora for Aquarius.

In interpreting the astrological meanings of ancient landscapes, one grows aware of their hidden histories, inscribed in their sacred places in a precise language of symbolism, which can be understood in any age by those, such as Jean Richer, whose intuition and capacity for dreaming are equal to their scholarship. The people who designed the landscape zodiacs were themselves dreamers, guided by necromancy and oracles. Dreams, it is said, are archetypal, conveying similar images to all people at all times. Richer's discovery of the Delphi zodiac was inspired by a dream, the same dream perhaps which caused the ancient Greeks to construct it, the dream of a divine order on earth, a reflection of the celestial zodiac.

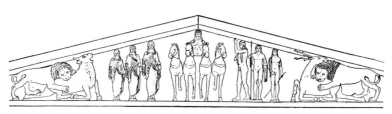

Fig. 35. The north-east pediment on the temple of Apollo at Delphi.

9

The sacred geography of continents: the St Michael-Apollo axis

The first and greatest of Jean Richer's discoveries, directly inspired by his dream at Athens in 1958, was the main axis of Greek sacred geography, the line through Delphi, Athens, Delos, Camiros, Apollo's temple at Prasaias, that of Artemis at Agra, the mystery centre at Eleusis and other sanctuaries. It links the main oracle sites of Greece, where the goddess first presided and where the cult of Apollo was later established. Statues and temples of Apollo at these places were usually accompanied by those of a goddess, often Athena, the patroness of Greece. The line marks the Virgo-Pisces axis of the zodiac centered on Delphi.

Naturally one is curious about possible further extensions of this emphatic alignment. Jean Richer, like most original scholars, was always too preoccupied with immediate researches to engage in calculations beyond his own field of study, and it fell to his elder brother, Lucien Richer, to make the astonishing discovery which opened a new dimension to archaeology and ancient history.

In the May-June 1977 number of the French journal, *Atlantis*, whose subject is 'scientific and traditional archaeology', Lucien Richer published a short article entitled 'The Saint Michael and Apollo axis'. He pointed to the fact that his brother's alignment of Apollo sanctuaries stretches south-eastward to Mount Carmel, the sacred mountain of the Canaanites in the Holy Land, while in the other direction, at an angle of virtually 60° west of north, it passes over the principal sanctuaries in Europe dedicated to the *36* Archangel Michael. From the site of the first recorded appearance of the Archangel in western Europe, Monte Gargano on the east coast of Italy, the line follows a sequence of similar apparitions, through Mont St Michel off the coast of Normandy and its sister islet, St Michael's Mount off the opposite coast of Cornwall, both

Fig. 36. The Apollo-St Michael axis of western Europe.

1 Skellig Michael.	8 Monte Sant'Angelo, Monte Gargano.
2 St Michael's Mount.	9 Kerkyras.
3 Mont St Michel.	10 Delphi.
4 Bourges.	11 Athens.
5 Sagra di San Michele.	12 Delos.
6 San Michele at Castiglione di	13 Lindos.
Garfagnana.	14 Mount Carmel.
7 Perugia.	

of them traditional places of St Michael visions, to the remotest of St Michael sanctuaries, the holy isle of Skellig Michael off the west coast of Kerry in Ireland. Another great St Michael sanctuary on this same line is the Sagra di San Michele in Piedmont in northwest Italy. To Richer's sites we can add another, the church of San Michele at Castiglione di Garfagnana, where a vision of the Archangel has been recorded.

Lucien Richer, since his retirement from a career in industry, has made a detailed study of this impressive alignment and is now writing a book on it. Therein will be disclosed his further discoveries of sanctuaries, significant legends and other aspects of the St Michael-Apollo axis. These additional details must await his own publication, but a discovery of such high interest, so relevant to our present theme, demands attention, and we therefore introduce it on the basis of what has so far been published and our own and other people's subsequent researches.

The first thing one wants to know about this line is its degree of accuracy when it is projected across the surface of the globe. Richer defines it as a line of constant bearing with the meridian, a so-called rhumb line, which can be represented on Mercator's projection of the globe by a straight line drawn between Skellig Michael and Mount Carmel. Richer writes that 'while each segment may not be orientated perfectly in the direction of 60° NW-SE, the differences are minimal and compensate for one another, so that the direction as a whole is indeed very close to this theoretic direction'. The true bearing from Mount Carmel to Skellig Michael is 60° 11'. Most of the alignments, he notes, 'are not purely linear but form a series of close parallels or, if one prefers, a more or less wide band'.

A mathematical survey of Richer's axis as a rhumb line was undertaken in 1986 by Robert Forrest. According to his calculations, the sacred places mentioned by Lucien Richer are placed as follows in relation to the theoretic rhumb line. The figures denote the distance in miles by which each site lies to the north of the line, minus values meaning that the site is south of it.

Skellig Michael	0
St Michael's Mount	8.9
Mont St Michel	10
Bourges	6.4
Sagra di San Michele	−8.3
Perugia	10.7
Monte Sant' Angelo, Monte Gargano	17.6
Kerkyras	−4.4
Delphi	−4.7
Athens	−0.6
Delos	3.6
Lindos	3.5
Mount Carmel	0

Bearing in mind the distance from the west of Ireland to the Holy Land, some 2500 miles, and the fact that many of the sites are natural landmarks, sanctified by nature rather than by human choice, the straight path on which they all stand is indeed narrow.

The appearance is of a *via sacra*, a sacred pathway between ritual centres which is a feature of ancient landscapes throughout the world, and this is supported by records of pilgrimage routes between places on the alignment.

Certain geographical and legendary features are common to many of these sites, often reflecting common attributes of the pagan Apollo and the Christian Archangel. St Michael's churches are typically on high, rocky crags or islets, where also is a spring and a mystical cavern. Temples to Apollo Delphinus, friend of the dolphin, also occur on promontories overlooking the sea, as at Acteum and the Athenian Acropolis rock, or on small islands such as Delos. Both St Michael and Apollo are symbols of spiritual revival, and both are dragon killers. Apollo slew Pytho, the previous, earth-serpent guardian of his Delphi shrine. His symbol there, the dolphin, identifies that aspect of the god with the sign of Pisces, and the line we are investigating forms the Virgo-Pisces axis of Jean Richer's Delphi zodiac. Its Virgo aspect is represented by the temples of Athena or of Artemis, Apollo's twin sister, which have an important place in the Apollonian sanctuaries, and by the chapels to the Virgin or some female saint which stand below the high places of St Michael. A frequent companion of the Archangel is the Christian saint whose legend identifies her most closely with Athena, Katherine of Alexandria.

A legend of Apollo is that soon after his birth he journeyed far north, to the land of the Hyperboreans, from where he returned to Greece. In following his path to the south-east, we begin our account of the stations on his route at the far Hyperborean sanctuary, Skellig Michael.

SKELLIG MICHAEL

Probably in pagan times, and certainly from the earliest days of Celtic Christianity, Great Skellig island off the coast of Kerry, $8\frac{1}{2}$ miles across stormy seas from the mainland at Valentia, has been a famous sanctuary. Formed of slate and old red sandstone, its extent is only 44 acres, and it rises 714 feet above the sea. There are three wells on the islet, geological faults have created fissures and caverns within it, and there is even said to be a long, underground tunnel from it, rediscovered and then blocked off by lighthouse keepers in about 1870.

37

Fig. 37. Skellig Michael, the ultimate holy rock of the Archangel off the west coast of Ireland.

The antiquity of the dedication to St Michael is unknown, but from at least as early as the sixth century the Archangel was patron saint of a Celtic monastery on the island rock. His reported apparition there, attended by the heavenly host, must have been early in the fifth century, for he is credited with helping St Patrick to clear Ireland of snakes and demons. The community was established on the only suitable ledge on the island, just below its summit. The impressive remains include six large dwellings with corbelled stone roofs, two oratories, a chapel, outbuildings, terraces and steps cut into the rock.

Little is known about the daily lives of the saints who inhabited this tempestuous outcrop. For weeks at a time during winter they would have been cut off from the mainland, and though they were no doubt adept at surviving on the herbs, fish and seafowl around them, their existence must have been highly rigorous and ascetic. Their sustenance was mostly spiritual, and the source of it is clearly shown by the main feature of their architecture, the sturdy, stone-roofed oratories. In these they performed their liturgies and chants, which enraptured their souls and extended the Christian enchantment of Ireland even to this loneliest rock. This incurred the jealousy of the Odinists. Early in the ninth century Vikings descended on the monastery, pillaged it and slaughtered the monks, and when the community was re-established, they returned several times with the intention of stamping it out.

The rock of Skellig Michael was a powerful attraction for pilgrims even from beyond Ireland. The difficult journey there from the Continent served as a penance for the most oppressive sins. A certain ritual was enjoined upon those who sought the Archangel's blessing. They had to climb almost to the summit and then edge along a spur of rock, the Needle's Eye, projecting out over the sea and ending with a carved rock which they had to kiss. Not all survived the ordeal. The story is told of a pilgrim who was heard, as he fell from the Needle's Eye, praying that the sea would rise up and end the agony of his fall.

By the nineteenth century, the tradition of fasts, vigils and religious services on Skellig island had degenerated into popular festivals. These became marked by practices which were considered scandalous, and the Church suppressed them.

St Michael's Mount

38   The island peak dedicated to St Michael in Mount's Bay, near Land's End in Cornwall, has the appearance of a small-scale replica of its sister rock off the opposite coast of Normandy. Its legends and early history are also much the same as those of Mont St Michel. Both mounts were formerly inhabited by giants. Those of Cornwall were said to have raised up the tors and crags of the western moorlands, and to one of them, Cormoran, is attributed the work of piling up the rocks of St Michael's Mount. He finally fell victim to a local giant killer, but he is still commemorated on the rock in the name of one of its wells, the Giant's Well.

At low tide St Michael's Mount can be approached by a cobbled
39   causeway from the coast at Marazion (Market Jew). At one time it was not an island but a rock in a wood, and remains of an ancient forest lie beneath the shallow waters of Mount's Bay. Legends of drowned lands tell of Lyonesse, the lost kingdom which once stretched westwards from Land's End as far as the Isles of Scilly. The date of the inundation is unknown, but if St Michael's Mount is identified as Ictys where, according to Roman writers,

traders from the Continent bought British tin, its insulation must have occurred in prehistoric times, for Ictys is described as an off-shore island.

The first-known inhabitants of the Mount were hermits dwelling in cells near the summit and probably maintaining a light for guiding seamen and travellers. The old histories give 495 as the year in which fishermen in Mount's Bay saw a glowing vision of the Archangel on a pinnacle of the rock. A Celtic monastery with a chapel to St Michael may have been built at about that time. It was replaced by a Benedictine abbey, founded by Edward the Confessor in 1044 and made subordinate to Mont St Michel after the Norman Conquest.

St Michael's Mount stands at the end of a pilgrimage route which passes along the south-western peninsula of Britain by a chain of hilltop sanctuaries dedicated to the Archangel. Those who made the journey to the Mount as a penance were expected to undergo an ordeal similar to that at Skellig Michael. At the top of the church tower is a rock known as St Michael's Chair. The pilgrims who conquered vertigo and climbed up to the Chair were assured of the Archangel's blessing. In preparation for the feat they would spend a night of vigil in the chapel of St Katherine which stood on a rock beside the causeway. From early times up to the Reformation, St Michael's Mount was as popular a resort for pilgrims as it is for tourists today.

MONT ST MICHEL

The most splendid of the Archangel's sanctuaries is the island mountain off the Normandy coast. St Michael himself ordered the *40* first of his churches to be built there. In 709 he appeared in a dream to St Aubert, Bishop of Avranches, and when the man ignored his instructions about the church, he marked the bishop's forehead with his finger as a sign that he meant to be taken seriously. St Aubert found the correct site indicated by a tethered bull, which had trampled the grass on the summit of the mount into a circle, but before a church could be built on that pattern, two large rocks had to be moved. A magic ritual was necessary for this, since the rocks were evidently two great menhirs of pagan sanctity, and this was effectively performed by a local peasant and his 12 sons. From that time, and especially after 966 when the

Figs. 38-41. Three of the rocky peaks or islets which stand on the Apollo–St Michael axis. This page: St Michael's Mount, Cornwall (*figs. 38 and 39*). Opposite: Mont St Michel in Normandy (*fig. 40*) and Sagra di San Michele in Piedmont (*fig. 41*).

Benedictine monastery was established there, Mont St Michel became one of the great pilgrimage centres of Christendom. All over Europe millennial hopes fastened themselves on St Michael, and in every period of spiritual revival waves of pilgrims made their way to St Michael's island mount. On the pinnacle of the church, built on the summit of the mount, a golden statue of the Archangel was visible from afar.

The early legends of Mont St Michel are interwoven with those of two other sanctuaries on the axis, the Cornish St Michael's Mount and Monte Gargano in Italy. St Michael's Mount is central to the British giant legends. As the tomb of a former giant it is called Tumba in the old histories, and Mons Tumba was the

Roman name for Mont St Michel. The Normandy mount is haunted by the legend of Gargantua, who has given his name to mountains and gorges through France, and also to Monte Gargano. He represents the elemental forces of the earth. Mons Tumba is the legendary burial place of his parent. Another of its early names was Mont Gargan.

The old pilgrimage path between Mont St Michel and Monte Gargano was trodden soon after the vision of 709 by two monks, sent by St Aubert to the Italian sanctuary with the request for relics of the Archangel. On their return they were amazed to see that Mons Tumba was no longer a rock in a forest but an island in the sea. During their absence Mont St Michel had been insulated by a flood, similar to that which had previously swamped the forests around St Michael's Mount.

Another legend of Mont St Michel links it not only with Gargano but also with Ireland. It tells how Ireland was being devastated by a foul dragon, and that the monster was finally killed by a miraculous sword which suddenly appeared among the people. Their archbishop was informed in a dream that the sword came from St Michael and should be restored to his favourite sanctuary on earth, which was assumed to be Monte Gargano. A party duly set out for there, bearing the sword. They passed by way of England into France, but when they tried to walk south to Italy, they found their steps directed westward. They prayed to the Archangel, who revealed to them that their proper destination was Mons Tumba. On arriving at Mont St Michel they were greeted by the abbot, and the miraculous sword was received into the monastery's treasure-house.

Before Mont St Michel gained its present name it is thought to have been one of the high sanctuaries of Belinus, the Celtic-Roman Apollo, whose name is echoed by that of Baal, worshipped on Mount Carmel. These dedications to gods of light and fire reflect certain natural properties of the sites. One of the most spectacular observations of earth light apparitions on the high places of St Michael took place at Mont St Michel in 1270, when the church on the summit appeared to be surrounded by flames.

Sagra di San Michele della Chiusa and San Michele in Garfagnana

41   The great monastery of San Michele, built on a seemingly inaccessible peak in Piedmont, north-west Italy, stands on the eastern ridge of the Alps, on the natural route into Italy from France. The spectacular site is said to have been chosen by the Archangel himself, who communicated his wishes through dreams and luminous visions. As at Mont St Michel there is a record of spiritual flames enveloping its summit. In the year 987 (or in some versions 999) a hermit on the nearby Monte Caprasio observed this mysterious fire, and took it as a sign that he should build a church to St Michael on the spot. It was called Monte Pirchiriano, Mount of the Lord's Fire, and the name of the hermit was Giovanni Vincenzo, a former archbishop of Ravenna and a pious scholar,

Fig. 42. At Le Puy in France is the most dramatic of St Michael sites, a church to the Archangel perched on the summit of a towering rock, the Needle.

who had grown so disturbed by his reputation for sanctity that he had become a mountain recluse.

Shortly afterwards, a nobleman from Auvergne, Hugh de Montboissier, was ordered by the Pope to build a church in expiation of some sin he had committed. On his way back from Rome he was told by St Michael in a dream that the church should be dedicated to him on Monte Pirchiriano. Since there was already a church there, Hugh began to build another on a neighbouring peak, but during the night the Archangel moved the stones to the site he had first indicated. Vincenzo's church was therefore replaced by another, more magnificent, and in a few years it became the most famous sanctuary in that part of Italy. At the height of its prosperity three hundred monks were lodged there and a perpetual round of chanting was maintained.

One of the legends of the monastery is of particular interest because it occurs also at another St Michael sanctuary, Le Puy in the Auvergne district of France, where an amazing rock formation, a tall, thin pinnacle, is topped by a church of St Michael. Apart

42

115

from local details, the two stories are the same: that a virgin leapt from the summit of the rock and was delivered safely to the ground by St Michael. This made her proud, and in order to show off she repeated her jump, but the second time there was no divine intervention and she was dashed on the rocks below.

Also on Richer's St Michael line we have located another sanctuary where the Archangel is said to have appeared. About two hundred miles beyond the monastery of San Michele della Chiusa, and some forty-five miles north-west of Florence, is the church of St Michael in the hilltop village of Castiglione di Garfagnana. Its legend is that a local man of sin, Bertone, was called to repentance by St Pellegrino. The message was backed up by a luminous apparition of St Michael on a rock above a rushing stream. Villagers on their way to the church used to interpret the howling of the wind as Bertone's penitent sighs and sobs.

MONTE SANT' ANGELO, MONTE GARGANO

If Italy is seen as a boot, Monte Gargano is its spur. It is a high, rocky headland, protruding into the Adriatic and belonging geologically to its opposite coast. In a former age it was an island, and in Roman times it was an isolated wilderness, a place of oak forests and sacred groves. Wolves roamed its heights, and bandits and outlaws found refuge there.

High up on the mountain is a cavern containing a sacred spring, and therein was a prehistoric shrine to the deities of earth, a subterranean place of initiation. In the year 492 – or in another version of the legend 390 – St Michael chose this place as the first of his sanctuaries in western Europe; as in the case of Mont St Michel he made his wishes known to the local bishop through a dream. It happened that a rich man of the district, named Garganus (a name which hints that in an earlier form of the legend he was a giant), lost one of his prize bulls and set out to look for it on the slopes of Monte Gargano. The animal was spotted high up the mountain at the entrance to a cave, and its owner was so angry with it that he shot at it with an arrow. The arrow turned in its course, flew back and wounded him. This prodigy was reported to the Bishop of Sipontium, a town to the south of Monte Gargano later called Manfredia. He ordered a general three-day fast, at the

Fig. 43. Cave painting at Monte Gargano, showing episodes in the legend of St Michael. The picture at the top left shows Garganus shooting at his strayed bull and being pierced in the eye by the returning arrow.

end of which the Archangel appeared to him saying that he was responsible for the returning arrow. It was meant as a sign that the cavern was to be his sanctuary and should be dedicated forthwith to St Michael. The bishop led a procession up the mountain, and within the cave they found an altar to St Michael, covered with a purple veil.

Shortly afterwards the shrine was attacked by the pagan Neapolitans. Again a fast was proclaimed, and the Archangel was called upon for advice. He ordered an attack, and as the battle began the mountain gave a mighty roar and belched flames upon the enemy. The pagans were routed and six hundred of them perished, mostly by flaming arrows loosed from an invisible bow. When the people went to give thanks at the Archangel's shrine, they found his footprint newly stamped on the marble altar.

During the following centuries, imitations of the mountain and cave sanctuary at Monte Gargano were fashioned all over Europe. Mont St Michel inherited much of its legend and was also presented

43

with two of its most valuable relics, the marble slab imprinted with the Archangel's foot and a feather which Satan detached from his wings during one of their battles. The fame of the Normandy mount grew to eclipse that of its parent, but in the eleventh century St Michael emphasized the importance of his senior shrine by appearing once more at Monte Gargano, this time to the Roman Emperor himself, Henry II. The Emperor had demanded to witness the Mass which the Archangel and his host were known to celebrate in the cave each night. This duly took place, but as a mark of his displeasure at the Emperor's intrusion, the Archangel touched him on his thigh and he was ever afterwards a cripple.

DELPHI AND THE GREEK-APOLLO LINE

The name of Delphi, meaning a cleft or vulva, presumably refers to the geological rift which once energized the famous earth oracle. Also heard in the name is *delphis*, a dolphin, and the dolphin was a symbol of Apollo in his Piscean aspect. When Apollo came to Delphi, the guardian of the oracle was Pytho, a worm-like creature described as the hideous offspring of Gaia the earth goddess. Apollo dispatched the monster with one of his darts, referred to by Aeschylus as whizzing, winged snakes. Thus he took possession of the oracle, whose prophetic utterances provided guidance to governments all over Greece. In the temple of Apollo was the omphalos stone with carved figures of the two eagles which Zeus released from the two ends of the earth. They met each other over Delphi, which was thus proved to be the centre of the world.

Nature rather than human choice selected Delphi as the most holy sanctuary of ancient Greece. Its awesome surroundings proclaim that here are located the earth's most powerful forces. It is a volcanic region, shaken by earthquakes. Mount Parnassus dominates it, and symbolic shapes in the rocks and peaks around it, when interpreted by the traditional code of geomancy, indicate a powerful range of planetary influences upon the site. Apollo's temple overlooks a valley, terminated by a conical mountain, and behind the temple are the horn-topped cliffs of the Phaedriades, the 'Brilliant Ones'. From between the two horns gushes forth the Castalian spring, and there also is the Corycian cave, 'bird-haunted and paced by gods'.

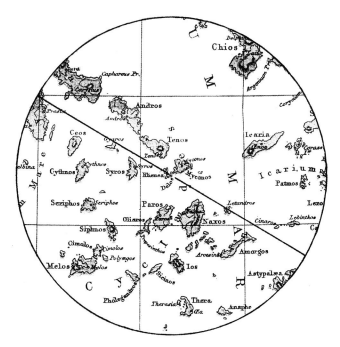

Fig. 44. Delos, the former centre of an ancient amphictyony, the birthplace of Apollo and the central hub of the Cycladic islands, forms one of the stations on the Apollo–St Michael axis.

We have referred earlier, in Chapter 2, to the twelve-tribe amphictyonies centred on Delphi, Athens and Delos. A pilgrimage route between these three main Apollonian sanctuaries more or less followed the line of the St Michael-Apollo axis. The other sacred places in Greece which Lucien Richer locates upon it are Kerkyras, the former Paleopolis, capital of the island of Corfu and the site of a famous temple to Artemis, and Lindos on Rhodes, where a high temple to Athena overlooks the sea.

The sanctuaries on this alignment have an overall consistency of character. Nominally they are ruled by Apollo or, in western Europe, by his Christian avatar, St Michael, but they are rooted in the power of the earth goddess, and that side of nature is expressed in its purest, sweetest form by the wise and virginal Athena. She and Apollo's sister, the lunar Artemis, have their temples beside those of the god on Apollo's axis of sanctity, and where St Michael dominates, chapels within his sanctuaries are

44

dedicated to St Katherine, Athena's Christian counterpart. The combination of the virgin goddess and the god whose favourite shrines are rocks in or above the sea supports Jean Richer's claim that this axis was ruled jointly by Virgo and Pisces.

MOUNT CARMEL

45 Carmel, a prominent sacred mountain of the Holy Land is mentioned in the fifteenth century BC, in the records of Thutmosis III of Egypt, as the Holy Head. The Carmel range terminates in a steep promontory jutting into the sea, the only one on the coast of Palestine, to form the southern end of the Bay of Acre. In prehistoric times it was covered in forests; hermits and prophets dwelt within its caves, and on its peaks stood temples and altars to a succession of ruling gods, Jehovah, Baal and Zeus. Tacitus says that the mountain was once sacred to a god, Carmel, who presided over an oracle there. The name means a garden, an image of paradise.

One of the holy sages who frequented Mount Carmel was Pythagoras. According to his biographer, Iamblichus in the fourth century, he travelled as a youth to Sidon, where he was initiated into the Phoenician mysteries, and then proceeded to Egypt for further studies. On the way he stopped at Mount Carmel, and spent some time in solitude at the temple of Zeus on its heights. There he encountered some Egyptian sailors who planned to sell him into slavery, but were deterred from molesting him by the god-like, gliding manner in which he descended the mountain.

A grotto in Mount Carmel, the Cave of the Sons of the Prophet, was inhabited by the prophet Elijah. On the edge of modern Haifa, it is still a place of prayer, sacred to Jews, Christians and Muslims. From ancient times it was famous for its healing properties. Lunatics were cured by spending three nights in it, and it was a resort of women who desired children. Nearby was the once famous oracle, consulted by the Emperor Vespasian before his siege of Jerusalem.

The story of how the worship of Baal on Mount Carmel was supplanted by the religion of Jehovah is told in I Kings 18. During the reign of King Ahab of Israel, an altar to Baal was erected on the heights. Elijah prophesied a drought, and then retired to the Cave of the Sons of the Prophet where he was fed twice a day by

Fig. 45. Mount Carmel, sacred at different times to Baal, Zeus and other gods of the elements, juts out from the coast of the Holy Land and forms the eastern terminus of the Apollo–St Michael axis.

ravens. The drought caused a terrible famine, and Elijah was ordered by God to approach Ahab with a promise to lift it if he would suppress the cult of Baal.

A magical contest was arranged between Elijah and 450 of the Baal priesthood. The traditional site, on the south-eastern tip of the Carmel range, is called El-Muhraka, the Place of Burning, and it took the form of a competitive fire invocation. Two sacrificial pyres of wood were set up, one for each side, and on each was placed a ritually slaughtered and dressed bullock. Whichever god produced fire to burn the sacrifice would be proclaimed the sole ruler of Israel.

All day long the priests of Baal called upon their god for fire, but even after they had worked themselves into a frenzy and slashed their bodies with knives, he made no answer. Elijah then rebuilt his altar, basing it on 12 stones to represent the 12 tribes of Israel, dug a trench round it and commanded 12 barrels of water to be poured over the sacrifice. He then prayed, 'and the fire of the Lord fell, and consumed the burnt sacrifice, and the wood, and the stones, and the dust, and licked up the water that was in the trench'. Jehovah was declared the winner and the priests of Baal were slaughtered.

Following the general path of the St Michael-Apollo axis, the Crusaders made for Mount Carmel and established below it their citadel port of Acre. In 1209 the first monastery of the newly founded Carmelite Order, claiming Elijah as its founder, was built near Elijah's fountain on the crest of the mountain ridge.

A LINE OF POWER AND VISION

Of the other western European sanctuaries which Lucien Richer locates on the St Michael-Apollo axis, Bruges is ancient Avaricum, the sacred centre of the Gallic tribe, the Bituriges; Perugia was one of the principal cities in an Etruscan twelve-city league. In addition, Richer has discovered the following sacred places on the straight line between Mont St Michel and Monte Gargano:

Pontmain, Mayenne, scene of an apparition of the Virgin Mary in 1871

Paray-le-Monial, Saône et Loire, where in the seventeenth century Marguerite Marie Alacoque had her famous visions of Christ which were the origin of the veneration of the Sacred Heart

Ars-sur-Formans, Ain, where between 1786 and 1859 lived the saintly Curé d'Ars, Jean-Baptiste-Marie Vianney

Assisi, the place of St Francis.

These places, in common with all the others in alignment with them, are distinguished by their associations with visions and visionaries. Richer has noted other such spots near the line of the St Michael-Apollo axis. The character of this line, he suggests, 'could be linked with one of the aspects of geomagnetism, which is thus revealed as a conveyor of spiritual energy'. Here again is a hint of that underlying mystery which dogs these researches. The idea which forms itself is of a vein in the vital energy field of the earth, a more or less straight channel from the west of Ireland to or through the Holy Land. At certain places the energy is released through crevices to the earth's surface, thus creating oracle centres, as at Delphi, Delos, Mount Carmel etc., elemental fire (Mont St Michel, Monte Sant' Angelo, Monte Gargano, Mount Carmel), visions of a glowing god or angel and apparitions of the Virgin. It is well known that forms of visions are determined by the cultural and religious background of the seer. Behind the details and interpretations of all such experiences is the same essential phenomenon: a magnificent glowing light is seen, and its witnesses are religiously inspired, often becoming saints, prophets, mystics or founders of churches.

A line across the earth which carries such power, inspiring visions to confirm the truth of the dominant religion; such a line, if recognized, would be of great value to a ruling priesthood. And there are plentiful indications that this line has been known, to pagan geographers, geomancers and missionaries of Apollo, to the esoteric philosophers of the early Celtic Church and to the inheritors of their mysteries, the mystical Christian orders, who promoted the Crusades and opened the way for Christian pilgrims on the sacred path to Mount Carmel and the Holy Land.

The St Michael-Apollo line has also been recognized by certain modern mystics, as is made clear in a guarded reference to it in an essay contributed to a booklet, *Michael, Prince of Heaven*, published in 1951. The writer, Margaret Thornley, spent the last active ten years of her life, up to 1957 when she was in her seventies, as a full-time pilgrim of St Michael. During that time she walked to more than 150 sacred places of the Archangel in Britain, Ireland and across the Continent. The legends of her travels include instances of levitation and luminous visions. The spirit of St Michael was her guide, and she acquired a deep insight into the nature of the angelic spirit and the mysteries of the high sanctuaries. 'The Pilgrim's Way', she wrote, 'winds onwards by the Mounts of Blessed Michael in Cornwall, Kerry and Brittany; down Europe to Carcassonne and Cousson, Lucca and Gargano, far away.' In linking these places, she defined the alignment from Skellig Michael off the coast of Kerry through the mounts of St Michael in Cornwall and Brittany to Monte Gargano. One of the other sites she mentions, the sanctuary of St Michael at Lucca in the west of Italy, is virtually in the same alignment. It may be that Margaret Thornley was unaware of the direct alignment of the principal St Michael sanctuaries, but their spiritual connection was clearly in her mind, and thus in a way she anticipated Lucien Richer's geographical discovery.

The earliest of the legends attached to the aligned St Michael sanctuaries are about giants. Examples include the legend of Cormoran who was supposed to have built St Michael's Mount and to be buried there, and Gargantua of Mont St Michel. In Geoffrey of Monmouth's twelfth-century *History of the Kings of Britain* is the story of how King Arthur sailed from Britain to Mont St Michel to kill an ogre who was terrorizing the neighbourhood from its summit. Garganus of Monte Gargano is reminiscent of the giant Polyphemus, who dwelt with his flocks and herds in a mountain cavern. Lucien Richer emphasizes the Cor-Gar-Car sound which links Mount Carmel and Monte Gargano with Gargantua and his giant tribe.

Giants are mythological symbols of the elemental forces within the earth. The bull, which features in the legends of both Monte Gargano and Mont St Michel, is also a symbol of earth energy. It naturally belongs to the Age of Taurus, covering some 2000 years from about 4000 BC, during which the priests and magicians of the megalith builders invoked the titanic forces of the earth.

At places which are associated with legends of giants and the powers of the underworld the earth's natural energies are at their most intense. Mystics tell of visions and strange lights seen at these places. These suggest a natural phenomenon, a form of luminosity which emanates from the earth during periods of geological stress, and also perhaps at times of spiritual intensity. There are several legends of flames or lights bursting spontaneously out of the earth, and the places where this happened being thereafter regarded as sacred. Churches and shrines were built on those spots, for they had shown themselves to be centres of sacred energy, where rites and invocations could most effectively be performed.

At a certain period in the development of nations, coinciding with the rise of their civilizations, worship of the earth spirit is replaced – or, rather, overlaid – by a solar theology, with Apollo or some corresponding solar deity as its leading principle. This is illustrated in the numerous accounts of a hero who killed a giant, dragon or monster, as Apollo slew the serpent at Delphi.

The general pattern of events at the St Michael sanctuaries appears to be that, first, these places were sacred rocks and island hills, where great people were buried and tribal initiations were held under the guidances of shamans who invoked the powers of earth. The earth spirit, properly symbolized by the mercurial serpent, became identified in Apollonian times with Satan as a poisonous worm or dragon. In piercing its head with a spear, the solar hero arrests its flow and fixes its energies in one spot. The

Figs. 46–47. St Michael, the radiant archangel who inherited attributes of Apollo, Woden and the Celtic Belinus, has authority over two worlds, above and below. As leader of the heavenly hosts he slays demons, dragons and earth monsters, and he is also the guide to the mysteries of death and the underworld. His main emblems are therefore the solar spear, shown in Dürer's *St Michael Quelling the Dragon* of 1498 (left), and the scales in which he weighs the qualities of dead souls, as depicted in this detail of Rogier van der Weyden's *The Last Judgment* of *c.* 1446 (below).

image is alchemical in origin, anterior to Christianity, and was probably associated with Mont St Michel and other such places when the Celtic Apollo ruled them. That god, known as Belinus in Gaul and Wotan in Germany, passed on many of his attributes to St Michael. Thus the Christian Archangel succeeded to the high sanctuaries where, as leader of the heavenly host, he is suitably

46 stationed to combat the demons of the upper air.

In one hand St Michael holds a golden sword and in the other a pair of scales, the latter symbolizing the other side to his character, as guide to the underworld. As Apollo took over the earth oracles, so did Michael become heir to the caverns of the earth spirit beneath the mountain sanctuaries. The earliest, eastern

47 shrines of St Michael are in grottoes. In his scales he weighs the souls of the dead, emphasizing their virtues over their vices and interceding on their behalf with the devil. All his various guises, as heavenly protector, initiator and friend to pilgrims, travellers and departing souls, are expressed in the composition of his favourite sanctuaries, typically an island mount in the west, with a beacon light on its summit, and below it a mystic cavern, leading to the nether regions of the earth.

The line we have followed, the continuation of the Virgo-Pisces axis through Delphi, is of particular relevance to the dawn of Christianity. With the Age of Pisces came Jesus, referred to esoterically as the Fish. In the astrological nativity of the Christian era, Pisces stands at the top of the chart with Virgo opposite and below it, illustrating the birth of Jesus as the Fish from Mary, who is *mare*, the sea. The coming of Christ is thus symbolized by the Virgo-Pisces axis, and the symbolism is completed by the events which took place along this axis during the early centuries of Christianity. A line of sacred places, formerly dedicated to Apollo or some local equivalent, was converted into a line of Christian sanctuaries, dedicated one after another to the warrior Archangel.

The mystery of how this came about is explained in no written history. An esoteric tradition is implied, a knowledge of ancient sacred geography possessed by initiates among the early Christians, and later guarded by mystical orders such as the Knights Templar. It was they who assumed the task of protecting pilgrims on the route from western Europe to Mount Carmel and the Holy Land, motivated perhaps by an initiated understanding of the St Michael-Apollo axis and its occult significance to Christianity. This knowledge was a secret of pagan religion, brought over into Christianity by mystical scholars of the early Church. The centre of traditional learning in early Christendom was Ireland, and from there, it is suggested, the Archangel Michael began his conquest of the high sanctuaries on the straight path leading to Mount Carmel.

Christianity, in its original mystical form, came to Britain from the East, and was merged in the Celtic Church with the traditions of Druidism. Michael, the prince and guardian angel of Israel, who spoke to Moses on the Mount, was adopted at an early stage in Celtic Christendom. In her book on St Michael, *Le Culte de Saint-Michel*, Olga Rojdestvensky traces the spread of his cult from Ireland to the Continent by Irish and Anglo-Saxon missionaries. The historian of Mont St Michel, Germaine Bazin, agrees with her in this, acknowledging the influence of monks from the British Isles in the foundation of St Michael's Norman sanctuary and of others throughout Europe. She points out that up to the sixth century the cult of the Archangel was unknown in Christian Gaul. Veneration was confined to local saints and martyrs, the apostolic fathers and founders of churches. It was, she says, a form of ancestor worship inherited from the Romans. The mystical tradition of Christianity was preserved by the Celts and Anglo-Saxons and entered Gaul from the North. With it came the light and energy represented by St Michael, inspiring the renaissance under Charlemagne and a flowering of Christian culture throughout western Europe.

A St Michael line
through England

48   A string of St Michael sites, similar in some ways to Lucien Richer's line through western Europe, was noticed by John Michell in 1967 and described in *The View Over Atlantis*. Since then it has been studied or experienced from various points of view by artists, mystics, dowsers, surveyors and others, and some interesting new features have been observed. The fact that it appeals to imaginative people today is itself interesting, for human nature is ever the same, and spiritual perceptions of modern times echo those of past ages. If this line of sanctuaries had not been of particular significance in antiquity, it could not have acquired the power of attraction which it now possesses.

50   A geographical peculiarity of this line is that it is the longest that can be drawn over dry land in southern Britain, for it stretches from the western tip of Cornwall at Land's End to where East Anglia bulges into the North Sea. Its point of balance, roughly half way along its course, is at the greatest of England's prehistoric temples, Avebury. Westwards from Avebury, the most spectacular of St Michael's hill and island sanctuaries fall either directly on the line or beside it.

    The axis of the line is defined very precisely by two Somerset hills, about ten miles apart, both topped by ruined churches to St
51 Michael. One is the famous landmark, St Michael's at Glastonbury Tor. The other, to the south-west at Burrowbridge, is called the
49 Mump, a reference to its bold, tumulus shape. Both of them rise out of flat countryside and were formerly surrounded by water to form island hills. The axis of the Mump is directed towards Glastonbury Tor, which is visible from its summit, and the axis of the Tor, together with the old Pilgrim's Way along its ridge, are on the same alignment. This alignment points directly to the main, southern entrance of Avebury.

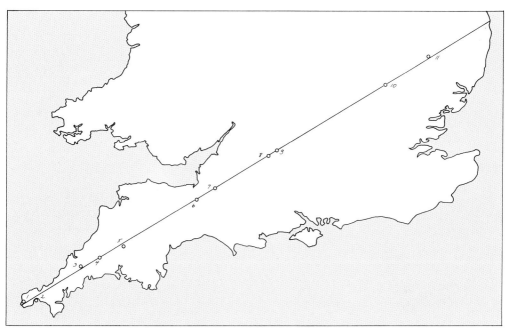

Fig. 48. Notable sanctuaries on or near the straight line of the St Michael axis between the eastern and western extremities of England include:

1 St Michael's, Carn Brea.
2 St Michael's Mount.
3 St Michael's Chapel, Roche Rock.
4 The Cheesewring.
5 St Michael's, Brentor.
6 St Michael's, Burrowbridge.
7 St Michael's, Glastonbury Tor.
8 Avebury.
9 St George's, Ogbourne St George.
10 Royston Cave.
11 Abbey, Bury St Edmunds.

Calculations by Robert Forrest prove that the line from St Michael's church on Burrowbridge Mump, through the church on the Tor and along the southern perimeter of Avebury's great stone circle, is perfectly straight across the earth's surface. Five miles east of Avebury the line goes through the centre of the ancient church at Ogbourne St George, once an important monastic site. St George is understood by some to be the earthly counterpart of St Michael.

Fig. 49. St Michael's church on Burrowbridge Mump.

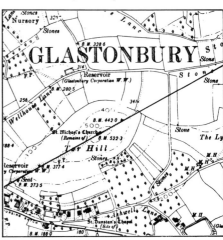

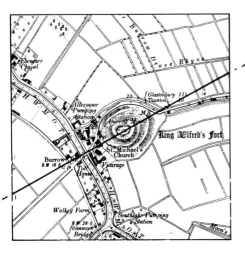

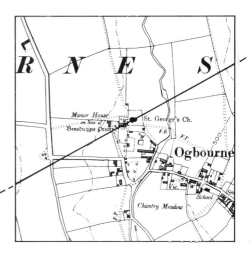

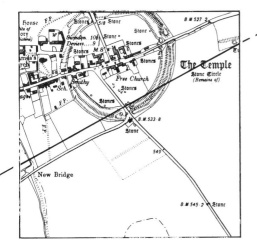

Fig. 50. The exact bearing of the
St Michael axis from its western terminus
at Land's End peninsula is defined by the
cluster of sites in its central section. From
the centre of Burrowbridge Mump to the
west, a straight line passes through
St Michael's tower on Glastonbury Tor
and the southern entrance stones of
Avebury to the ancient church site at
Ogbourne St George.

Fig. 51. Glastonbury Tor.

Fig. 52. The Cheesewring, a marker on the St Michael line.

Opposite: *Fig. 53.* St Michael's church on the rock at Brentor.

Extended westward, the line runs straight to an outstanding ancient landmark on Bodmin Moor in Cornwall, a towering pile 52 of rocks known as the Cheesewring. On the way to its terminus at Land's End it passes within sight and easy reach of the following St Michael sanctuaries:

53 St Michael's, Brentor. Perched on top of a steep volcanic cone of granite, overlooking Dartmoor to the east, this tiny church to the Archangel of the high places served as a landmark for ships off the north Devon coast. In former times it was probably a beacon hill. Prehistoric walls, protecting its lower slopes, indicate ancient sanctity. Legend says that, while the church was being built, the devil kept removing its stones, until St Michael appeared and knocked the devil down with a rock, which is still there at the foot of the hill.

St Michael's rock chapel and hermitage, Roche. Rising out of level moorland to the north of St Austell in Cornwall is a tall rock formation with a hermit's cell and a chapel carved into its peak. At its foot is a holy well. The hermitage was occupied up to the thirteenth century, and there are legends of Celtic saints who lodged there.

St Michael's Mount, described more fully on pages 110–11, lies about three miles south of the direct line from Avebury to Land's End, but it was the main goal of pilgrims along the line of St Michael stations to the far west. Here the line intersects the alignment of St Michael sites through western Europe.

St Michael's, Carn Brea. Most of the prominent hilltops in Cornwall are dedicated to St Michael, a tradition which goes back to the time of the Celtic Church. Carn Brea, near the western end of the line, is the first or last in the chain of beacon hills through the West Country. Up to the nineteenth century a chapel to St Michael, built upon a prehistoric chambered mound, stood on top of it.

Having established the true bearing of this line, Robert Forrest listed the old churches which stand either on or just off it. Within a band 550 yards on either side of the central axis he found a total of sixty-three churches between Land's End and the East Anglian coast. Ten of them were dedicated to St Michael or St George, and over a third of them, twenty-three in all, were churches of St Mary. This parallels Richer's finding of shrines to the Virgin between the high sanctuaries of St Michael.

Since 1988 a detailed study of this alignment has been undertaken by two followers of the earth spirit, residents of Cornwall. Paul Broadhurst is the author of *Secret Shrines*, on the mystical traditions of Cornwall's holy wells, and his partner, Hamish Miller, is a dowser from Scotland. In the course of travelling between the St Michael sites from Land's End up to and beyond Avebury, they have detected two continuous threads of earth current, which meander around the straight axis of the line, passing through many of the churches and sacred monuments on either side of it and creating spiral patterns at the major sanctuaries on its route. Their book on this phenomenon, *The Sun and the Serpent*, was published in the autumn of 1989.

The picture which they give is of a straight rod along the spine of southern England, around which twists a coil of terrestrial energy. It illustrates a concept in traditional eastern medicine, of vital currents moving serpent-fashion between the nodal points in the energy field of the body. Chinese geomancers have the same perception of the flow of energies in the body of the earth. This pattern is represented by a staff with snakes curling round it, an emblem of Asclepius, the Greek god of healing, and also by the caduceus, the rod entwined by two serpents which is an attribute of Hermes. In that symbol is a clue to the nature of the line we are investigating. Hermes stands for an earlier, less civilized aspect of deity than Apollo. He is identified with the mercurial spirit of the earth, and thus he brings intelligence and inspiration and introduces neophytes to the subterranean mysteries. Never fixed, ever flowing, he is the guide of travellers and pilgrims. The light of his spirit flickers over the sacred heights and haunts the paths between them. Hermits who attend a beacon light are his special servants.

The serpentine energy flow which the dowsers from Cornwall have followed up to Avebury is surely a natural phenomenon, but the straightness of its axis is clearly artificial. Of the landmarks in precise alignment from Land's End, only Glastonbury Tor is indisputably a work of nature. Burrowbridge Mump, though far larger than any prehistoric tumulus that has yet been recognized, has certain signs of being manmade, and the status of the Cheesewring has long been disputed. Early antiquarians thought it was constructed as an idol by an ancient priesthood, while legend attributes it, perhaps more plausibly, to the Cornish giants.

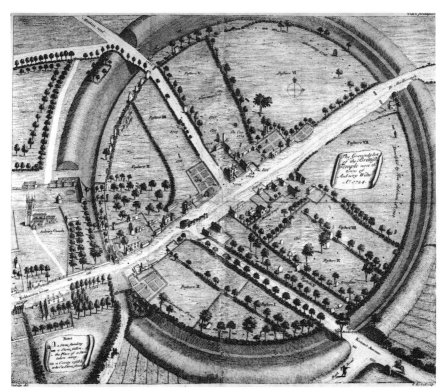

Fig. 54. William Stukeley's ground plan of Avebury in 1724. The St Michael line passes through the large stones at the southern gateway, where the Kennett Avenue enters the rings. An old stretch of road continues the line to the west.

These landmarks form the pole around which the serpent current winds on its path to the temple at Avebury, and at Avebury is the serpent's head. Built in a vale at the sources of two rivers, at the meeting-place of earth currents from different quarters of England, it is regarded by dowsers as a powerful centre of energy. Two curving avenues of standing stones, one of them now destroyed, converged upon the temple. William Stukeley in his eighteenth-century *Abury Described* called them serpents, and he was the first to identity Avebury as a serpent temple, shaped as an alchemical *54* symbol of divine power. On the font at Avebury's church is an early stone carving of a bishop transfixing a serpent with his crozier.

If the Cheesewring and Burrowbridge Mump are indeed artificial, they must be far older than the works of the megalith builders and form part of an earlier, more gigantic system of geomancy. There is an air of great antiquity about the line they stand on. No doubt it was once a pilgrimage route. Stretches of an ancient pathway lie upon or parallel to it, such as the Pilgrims' Way over Glastonbury Tor and the road approaching Avebury from the west. Further east it picks up sections of the prehistoric Icknield Way. This path between the chain of St Michael hills formed the natural route for the tribes of the West Country in their progress up to Avebury for the annual midsummer fair. Their landmarks were the high places, where beacon fires guided the travellers by night. A Celtic Hermes was their guiding deity. The road wandered past wayside shrines and places of refreshment, following the currents of serpent energy.

Major arteries of earth current in China are called dragon lines, probably because of the luminous phenomena which sometimes appear over them. Lights and apparitions are also associated with the St Michael hills. The record extends from the fifth-century vision of the Archangel on St Michael's Mount to periodical sightings of mysterious lights over Glastonbury Tor and Avebury. Modern folklore links these lights with extra-terrestrial spacecraft, but generally they appear to be natural rather than constructed objects. Those seen over Glastonbury Tor have been compared to fireflies or luminous shoals of fish. They hover, dart and make sudden changes of course in the manner of disembodied energy.

Paul Devereux has studied this phenomenon, and in two recent books, *Places of Power* and *Earth Lights Revelation*, has assembled much evidence, from archaeology, geology, physics, local history and his own fieldwork to produce a general theory of 'earthlights' and their connection with sacred places. Experiments with magnetometers and other instruments prove that the sites of stone circles are anomalies in the earth's energy field. The levels of radiation there are markedly different from those of their immediate surroundings. Geological fault lines run below or near every stone circle. The rocks beneath the earth at those places are under friction, and this produces an electrical discharge which is sometimes briefly visible in the form of lights on or above the surface of the earth. To this effect Devereux attributes many of the wraiths, phantoms and weird lights which occur in traditional folklore, as well as in modern experience, at spots of ancient sanctity.

This does not altogether explain the mystery; in fact it deepens it, for, as Devereux points out, there is a psychic dimension to earthlights. Their appearance seems to induce in some people a state of vision, and it is associated with periods of religious revival as in the outbreak of religious fervour which took place in North Wales early in 1905. Preachers arose and people flocked to the chapels, many of them seeing strange lights and luminous forms. The most widely reported sightings of moving lights around Glastonbury Tor, over a few years from 1967, coincided with a time of visions and millennial excitement in the district. At about the same period in nearby Warminster, groups of UFO enthusiasts assembled nightly on hilltops to observe lights floating above them. Encounters with strange entities were reported, and many people believed in approaching revelations from space beings. Warminster, Glastonbury Tor and the scene of the Welsh apparitions in 1905 are in areas of geological faulting.

With lights and visions come other strange phenomena. At Avebury in the summer of 1988 a light in the sky was seen shining down on to Silbury Hill, and next morning an impression of geometrically arranged rings and circles was discovered on a neighbouring cornfield. Throughout that summer similar markings were observed in crops over southern England, and those who investigated them experienced the type of excitement which is often generated by psychic events. Many of the crop marks were by ancient monuments, and several have recurred at the same spots over a number of years.

Terrestrial stigmata, aerial lights, apparitions and revivalist movements appear in some way to be interrelated, and one of the links between them is topographical. Avebury and Glastonbury are at strong centres of the energy line which the dowsers have traced from Cornwall. Both places in very early times had a reputation for sanctity, which extended down the pilgrimage path westward to St Michael's Mount. This is also the path of a vital current, connected by nature with the human psyche and formerly identified with the mystical light and spirit of Hermes. The traditional significance of this path is indicated by an item of lore, recorded by Wellesley Tudor Pole. In a booklet published in 1951, *Michael, Prince of Heaven*, he mentions a saying in the villages of West Somerset, that one day Jesus Christ will walk again along the path from Cornwall to Glastonbury, and when he comes the villagers must recognize and entertain him.

PART III

II

The chorography of nations

In all the 12-tribe leagues or amphictyonies which we have so far described the general rule is that the members of each league are of the same ethnic group with a common religion, language and culture. An intriguing development of this idea is hinted at in the traditional practice of chorography. The word comes from the Greek for *Choros*, a country or region, and it was formerly used much as topography is now, to denote the charting of a region together with the features and character of its various parts. Ancient chorographies were largely concerned with astrology, each country or district being placed under a zodiacal sign. Natural forms in the landscape, such as rivers, mountain ranges and coastlines, were sometimes drawn so as to emphasize their resemblance to human or animal figures. This tradition, which has its roots in geomancy, is represented in modern times by those whimsical maps which show, for example, the British Isles as the profile of an old woman holding her fractious baby Ireland.

Implied by the old chorographies is the existence of wider organizations than the one-nation amphictyonies, the existence of 12-nation leagues, speaking perhaps several different languages and with different customs in each country, but held together by a religious system which placed each nation under a particular constellation and allotted it to one of the 12 gods. Behind this is the vision of a universal brotherhood, a peaceful union of mankind. That vision recurred at the beginning of Christianity, as illustrated by the Pentecostal chorography in figure 56. To the early Christians the unifying bond between all nations was to be the faith in Christ, but an earlier source of brotherhood may be indicated by the alternative meaning of the word, chorography, a version of choreography, meaning the composition of a dance. A tradition of the Greek amphictyonies is that they were originally choral associations of 12 tribes, and a chorography may therefore be seen as a dance of nations with music as their common bond.

The existence throughout Greece and the ancient world of leagues made up of 12 tribes or cities suggests a wider astrological union, embracing the entire human race, or those members of it who were known to the old geographers of the Near East. Such a concept is indeed apparent in the works of ancient authors, and it occurs in the New Testament, in the Acts of the Apostles, usually attributed to St Luke the Evangelist, who was an artist, physician and companion to St Paul in his missionary journeys through Asia Minor.

In the second chapter of Acts is the story of Pentecost, when the 12 Apostles, with Matthias in the place of Judas Iscariot, were assembled together in Jerusalem. Suddenly the room was filled with the sound of a rushing wind; a luminous spirit like a flame settled on each of the Apostles, and they began to speak in tongues. This marvel attracted the multitude, and crowds of people from every nation on earth hurried to witness it. The Apostles were Galileans, but every member of the crowd heard them speaking in his own native language. Some people cried out that the Apostles must be drunk, but St Peter stood up and claimed that the event was nothing less than the fulfilment of that most beautiful and inspiring of prophecies, uttered by the prophet Joel:

And it shall come to pass in the last days, saith God, I will pour out my Spirit upon all flesh; and your sons and your daughters shall prophesy, and your young men shall see visions, and your old men shall dream dreams:

And on my servants and on my handmaidens I will pour out in those days of my Spirit; and they shall prophesy:

And I will show wonders in heaven above, and signs in the earth beneath; blood, and fire, and vapour of smoke:

The sun shall be turned into darkness, and the moon into blood, before that great and notable day of the Lord come:

As the result of St Peter's rousing sermon, in which he promised salvation and the gift of the Holy Spirit to those of any nation who were baptized, some 3000 people were converted to Christianity.

The list of peoples who were present at the first Pentecost is given in Acts 2: 9–11:

Parthians, and Medes, and Elamites, and the dwellers in Mesopotamia, and in Judaea, and Cappadocia, in Pontus, and Asia, Phrygia, and Pamphylia, in Egypt, and in the parts of Libya about Cyrene, and strangers of Rome, Jews and proselytes, Cretes and Arabians, we do hear them speak in our tongues...

This story was one of the bases of a legend, current in the early Church and referred to in Eusebius's fourth-century *Church History*, that the 12 Apostles divided the world into twelve regions and then drew lots to decide which region each of them should take as his mission field. The tradition of chorographies, in which each part of the world is placed under one of the twelve astrological signs, goes back to ancient Egypt and Babylon. Drawing on many early sources, Paul of Alexandria in his *Eisogogue* of 378 AD compiled an astrological register of countries which has many similarities with the list of nations given in the Acts. They are compared below.

Zodiac	Paul of Alexandria	Acts
1 Aries	Persia	Parthians, Medes, Elamites
2 Taurus	Babylon	Mesopotamia
3 Gemini	Cappadocia	Cappadocia
4 Cancer	Armenia	Pontus
5 Leo	Asia	Asia
6 Virgo	Hellas & Ionia	Phrygia & Pamphylia
7 Libra	Libya & Cyrene	Libya & Cyrene
8 Scorpio	Italy	Rome
9 Sagittarius	Cilicia & Crete	Cretanus
10 Capricorn	Syria	Judaea
11 Aquarius	Egypt	Egypt
12 Pisces	Red Sea & India	Arabs

The authorities generally agree that Judaea is a late addition to the list of lands mentioned in Acts. Bouché-Leclerq, the late nineteenth-century historian of astrology, found that Paul of Alexandria's list made geographical sense as far as Italy, which both Manilius and Dorotheus equated with Libra. He said that Paul did Italy an injustice in placing it under Scorpio, and that the

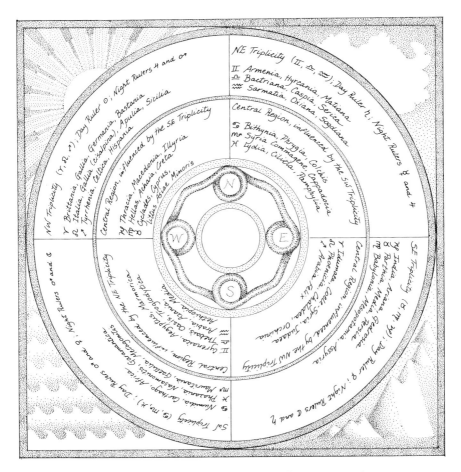

Fig. 55. Ptolemy's chorography, a symbolic grouping of nations according to astrological and geomantic considerations.

rest of his series was an attempt to match astrological signs with the temperaments of the various native peoples. Paul was also concerned to follow as far as possible the order of a previous chorography, that of Ptolemy. Paul's list was therefore a compromise.

Ptolemy's system, which we show in diagrammatic form in figure 55, is the most complex of all chorographies. Countries are grouped to form triplicities under the signs corresponding to earth, air, fire and water. It is not easy to reconcile Ptolemy's arrangement with actual geography, but he is still taken as the authority by modern practising astrologers. Those of the traditional school consult it when making readings for a state, region or society whose foundation date is unknown.

The attribution of zodiacal signs to geographical regions comes earlier in the history of astrology than the individual natal chart. The earliest astrology was closely linked to geomancy, and was used, among other things, to give warnings to the authorities of portended events, such as eclipses, social disturbances, floods, famines, earthquakes and wars.

56   In figure 56 we have reconstructed the chorography of Pentecost. The zodiac is aligned with the spring sign, Aries, to the east, and the list of nations is read in reverse order to that given in Acts, beginning with the Arabs (Red Sea and India) who are under the sign of Pisces. This is appropriate because the beginning of the Age of Pisces coincided with the birth of Christ. The circle follows the sun anti-clockwise in its regression through the zodiac. Egypt under Aquarius comes next, after which, apart from the difficulties with Judaea and Italy mentioned above, the various nations fall more or less under their appropriate signs. The circle ends with the Parthians, Medes and Elamites, dwelling in their proper region under Aries. There are certain anomalies, as with Mesopotamia which lies mostly outside its Taurus sector, but we note that Taurus contains the upper reaches of the Tigris and Euphrates, the rivers which, as it were, put Mesopotamia on the map. Other correspondences turn out to be more accurate than they at first appear. Asia looks poorly defined within the Leo sector, but the reference of course is to Asia Minor, the north-west part of which was in early Christian times, a Roman province. It is reassuring to find that India is in fact located where Paul of Alexandria placed it, under Pisces.

For this wheel of nations to make geographical sense, its centre must be located in Asia Minor, and experiments show that it works best in the region of Sardis, the ancient capital of Lydia. This once great religious and commercial centre is mentioned in Revelation as one of the seven churches of Asia. Here it appears as the world centre of a traditional pattern of sacred geography, linking together people of many different cults and customs under a pantheon of twelve gods whose images were in the stars. Behind the reference to this system in the Acts of the Apostles can be discerned the aspiration of many early Christians, to see the ancient science restored in the name of Christ and the twelve Apostles.

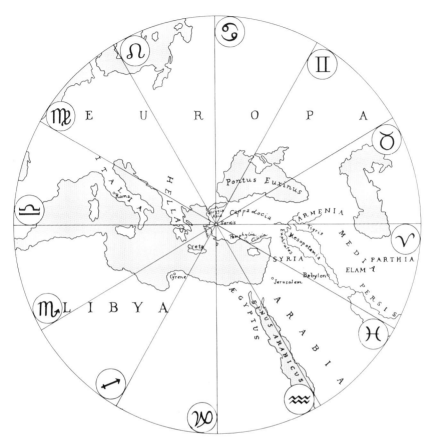

Fig. 56. The ancient tradition of a chorography of 12 nations, placed within a zodiac and united by an astrological religion, was revived through the Christian revelation. The list of nations represented at the first Pentecost is shown in the above diagram. After the Crucifixion, the 12 Apostles, whom Constantine at the Nicean Council identified with the 12 zodiacal signs around Christ the Sun, divided the known world between themselves, each taking one of the 12 sections as his mission field.

A feature of this zodiac which must have been apparent to early Christian scholars is its relevance to world history. During the astrological age preceding Pisces, that of Aries, the most powerful nations were those of Persia and the Middle East, where the teachings of Zoroaster gave new life and expression to the ancient wisdom. In the zodiac Persia and imperial Babylon are placed in the Aries sector. With the dawn of Pisces, the Piscean sector became illuminated, and under Pisces is Arabia and the Holy Land. Jerusalem, at the centre of the Piscean sector, was to be the holy city throughout that age for the three religions which dominated it, Jewish, Christian and Muslim. Mecca is also in that sector. As the Piscean Age gives way to Aquarius, the sun crosses the Red Sea and enters Egypt. Ancient Egypt is rising again within the Aquarian mind, and the Great Pyramid has become a popular symbol and reminder of the ancient sacred science.

Our location of Sardis as the apparent centre of a traditional 'amphictyony of all nations' coincides with the identification by Jean Richer of a zodiac, the very same as in our figure 56, also centred on Sardis. Of all the landscape zodiacs which he has investigated he believes this to be the oldest.

The first clue which led Richer to Sardis was the unusual orientation of Apollo's temple at Camiros on Rhodes, one of the main axis lines through Delphi, Athens and Delos. The temple, which is orientated due north, points to Sardis, and this alignment forms one of the spokes in its zodiac wheel.

Sardis has many of the attributes of a symbolic world centre. It was dedicated to the ancient goddess, and its temple of Artemis was the national sanctuary of Lydia and the probable meeting-place of a 12-tribe amphictyonic council. Vincent Scully, with his perceptive eye for symbolism in sacred landscapes, was struck by the natural qualities of its site. He describes its sacred mountain, the Acropolis, as 'magical and barbarous, savage in scale'. The highest peak of Mount Tmolus, which dominates the approach to Artemis's temple, is shaped as a perfect lunar crescent, the universal landscape symbol of the goddess, and the temple's axis is aligned upon a mighty, pyramidal rock, resembling Mount Kailas. As Kailas through its shape and position is a natural image of Mount Meru, the mythical mountain at the world centre, so also is this mountain at Sardis.

The legends and artefacts of Sardis echo the symbolism of its landscape. Its early coins, like those of Delphi, show a serpent entwined around its symbolic centre, the omphalos, which at Sardis took the form of a *cista mystica*, resembling the Ark of the Covenant. The word omphalos is heard in the name of its legendary queen, Omphale. She bought Hercules as a slave from Hermes after he had completed his 12 labours, and set him to work at her spinning wheel, representing the revolving wheel of the zodiac.

The ruling deity of Lydia was the goddess, whose many-breasted statue stood in the temple of the Sardian Artemis and in many

57

Fig. 57. Framed by the ruins of the temple of Artemis-Cybele, this pyramid-shaped rock above Sardis forms a natural symbol of Mount Meru, the world centre mountain. It stands at the centre of the zodiacal diagram (*fig. 56*).

other sanctuaries throughout Asia Minor. The carved vestments and ornaments of those statues which survive are full of astrological symbolism. In many of them the goddess is wearing an astrological necklace made up of zodiacal signs. Richer states that the sign which is placed centrally on her breast refers symbolically to the region where the statue was erected. Most perfect of these statues is *La belle Artemis*, now in the Museum at Ephesus. She is an image of that statue which fell from Jupiter, mentioned in Acts 19, whose devotees howled down St Paul's missionary party with cries of 'Great is Diana of the Ephesians!'. Her necklace of zodiac signs has Scorpio in the centre, and in Richer's interpretation of the Sardis zodiac Ephesus is in the Scorpio sector. There is a discrepancy here between Richer's reading of the zodiac and the version that emerges from the Acts. Both Richer's and ours look the same, but our evidence is that the signs must be read in celestial

58

Fig. 58. The statue of Artemis at Ephesus with
zodiacal necklace.

order, following the precession of astrological ages, from Aries to
Pisces, to Aquarius and so on, while Richer takes them in the
reverse, terrestrial order. The signs are placed on the same axes in
both versions, but Richer makes them dominate the sector adjacent
to them anti-clockwise, whereas ours run clockwise. It is nonethe-
less striking that two different approaches and two different sets
of clues should have led to the same conclusion, that Sardis was
the hub of a zodiacal wheel which contained the nations of the
ancient world.

The twelve tribes of Israel and the sacred geography of the Holy Land

THE STORY OF THE TWELVE TRIBES

The most widely known amphictyony of 12 tribes is that of the tribes of Israel, whose right to possess the Holy Land was given to them by their god Jehovah. The story of how they received their Law upon Mount Sinai, and of their wanderings, captivities and wars of conquest, is a principal theme in the Old Testament, and it is a story which continues into the future. For the same scriptural prophecies, which have inspired the return of the Jews (traditionally identified as Judah, Benjamin and part of Levi) to their ancestral homeland, proclaim that one day all 12 tribes will be reunited at Jerusalem. The circle of their 12-part chant, which Jehovah gave to Moses (Deuteronomy 31:19), will then be complete, leading to that promised restoration when harmony under divine law will again be established on earth.

The Israelites are not the only 12-tribe amphictyony to have arisen in the Holy Land. In Genesis are mentioned 12 tribes of the Arameans (22: 20–24) and of the Edomites (36: 10–14), and other such groupings are hinted at. In the time of Mohammed, the Saracens and Nabataeans formed 12 tribes, each under one of the signs of the zodiac. Most important are the 12 sons of Ishmael, Abraham's only son by the Egyptian servant woman, Hagar. Their mother was also Egyptian, and they became princes of 12 tribes whose descendants are the Arabic nations. Thus they also have a traditional claim to the Holy Land. An inspired constitutionalist seems to be needed to reconcile the 12 tribes of Israel with their cousins, the Ishmaelites, in the country on which they have both set their hearts.

Before the days of the 12 tribes there were 12 patriarchs, two versions of whose names are given in Genesis 4 and 5. Like the gods and heroes of the Chaldeans, Phoenicians, Persians and many

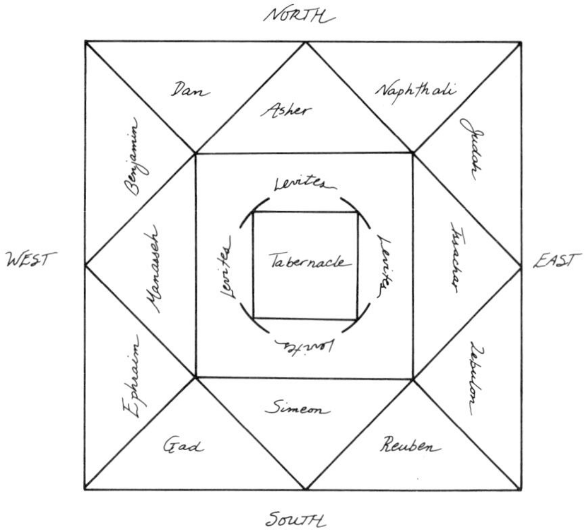

Fig. 59. The order of
encampment in the
wilderness as indicated in
Numbers 2. The 12 tribes
of Israel formed an
astrological system, but the
correspondence between
the tribes and the zodiacal
signs has never been
precisely established.

other peoples, they corresponded to the seasons, months of the
year and the signs of the zodiac.

The origin and development of the league of Israelite tribes are
in many ways similar to those of 12-tribe amphictyonies elsewhere.
The story began with divine revelation, when Jehovah gave the
Law to Moses. Included in the revelation were the song, implying
a canon of sacred music, and standards of proportion in the form
of 'a perfect and just measure' (Deuteronomy 25: 15). These and
other symbols of the Law were kept in the Ark, fashioned by
Moses to Jehovah's specifications.

Newly reformed into 12 tribes and nourished by Jehovah, the
Israelites roamed the wilderness for forty years, representing the
nomadic stage of their history. Wherever they camped, they pitched
their tents to form a square around the tabernacle containing the
Ark, each tribe taking its allotted position, three to each side of
the square with the Levites guarding the central tabernacle. The
order of encampment was astrological, for from the time when
they received the Law, each tribe corresponded to a zodiacal sign,
which may have been emblazoned on their tribal banners. Clues
to the signs which belonged to the various tribes are given in
Genesis 49, where Jacob calls his 12 sons together to bless or curse
them as he saw fit. Some of the prophetic phrases in which he
addresses them have obvious zodiacal symbolism. They were
interpreted in the seventeenth century by Athanasius Kircher, the

TRIBE	MEANING OF NAME	MOTHER	DESCRIPTION IN GENESIS 49	KIRCHER'S ASTROLOGICAL ATTRIBUTION
1 Reuben	'behold a son'	Leah ('weary')	'Reuben, thou art my firstborn, my might, and the beginning of my strength, the excellency of dignity, and the excellency of power: Unstable as water, thou shalt not excel...'	♒
2 Simeon	'hearing'	Leah	'Simeon and Levi are brethren; instruments of cruelty are in their habitations...Cursed be their anger...I will divide them in Jacob, and scatter them in Israel.'	♓
3 Levi	'joined'	Leah	See Simeon. Note: This tribe is not that of the priestly Levites. Simeon and Levi massacred all males in Shechem to avenge the violation of Dinah.	
4 Judah	'praised'	Leah	'Judah, thou art he whom thy brethren shall praise: thy hand shall be in the neck of thine enemies; thy father's children shall bow down before thee. Judah is a lion's whelp...'	♌
5 Dan	'judging'	Bilhah (Rachel's handmaid)	'Dan shall judge his people...Dan shall be a serpent by the way, an adder in the path, that biteth the horse heels, so that his rider shall fall backward.'	♏
6 Naphthali	'wrestling'	Bilhah	'Naphthali is a hind let loose: he giveth goodly words.'	♍
7 Gad	'troop'	Zilpah (Leah's handmaid)	'Gad, a troop shall overcome him: but he shall overcome at the last.'	♈
8 Asher	'happy'	Zilpah	'Out of Asher his bread shall be fat, and he shall yield royal dainties.'	♎
9 Issachar	'an hire'	Leah	'Issachar is a strong ass couching down between two burdens: And he saw that rest was good, and the land that it was pleasant; and bowed his shoulder to bear, and became a servant unto tribute.'	♋
10 Zebulon	'dwelling'	Leah	'Zebulon shall dwell at the haven of the sea; and he shall be for an haven of ships...'	♑
11 Joseph	'adding'	Rachel ('sheep')	'Joseph is a fruitful bough; even a fruitful bough by a well; whose branches run over the wall: The archers have sorely grieved him, and shot at him...But his bow abode in strength...'	♉
12 Benjamin	'son of the right hand'	Rachel	'Benjamin shall ravin as a wolf: in the morning he shall devour the prey, and at night he shall divide the spoil.'	♐
Manasseh, 'he that forgets', and Ephraim, 'double land', are not mentioned in Genesis. They were both of the root tribe of Joseph.				♊

Fig. 60. The astrological attributions of the 12 tribes.

149

60
Jesuit scholar whose insight into such esoteric matters has rarely been equalled. Figure 60 gives the names of the tribes in order of their birth, the meaning of their names, the names of their mothers, the significant phrases applied to them in Genesis 49 and Kircher's astrological attributions.

Many people have tried to discover a consistent link between the tribes and the signs, but the only fixed element in the scheme seems to have been the number 12. Throughout the Bible the tribes are never mentioned more than once in precisely the same order and with the same membership. Levi, which became the priestly tribe, is sometimes included in the 12, sometimes not. Manasseh and Ephraim, both stemming from the root tribe of Joseph, are sometimes counted as one tribe, and there are other variations. It is generally agreed that Judah, Reuben, Dan and Ephraim marked the four quarters, but elsewhere there is flux. This was also the case with other amphictyonic leagues in Greece and Italy. Sometimes the number of their members grew beyond the prescribed 12, but that number was religiously upheld, with some of the tribes sharing the rights and duties of league membership.

When the tribes crossed the Jordan from the east to begin their conquest and settlement of the Promised Land, they claimed possession of it in the name of Jehovah through certain geomantic rituals. Jordan's waters were miraculously rolled back, and where the bearers of the Ark stepped on to its west bank, a circle of 12 stones was erected (Joshua 4). The tribes were also instructed (Deuteronomy 27) to put up another circle of 12 stones on Mount Ebal which, with its neighbour, Mount Gerizim, marks the geographical centre of the Holy Land. The stones were to be smoothly plastered and inscribed with the words of the Law. Also prescribed was a strange ritual of blessing six tribes from Mount Gerizim and cursing the other six from Mount Ebal. The plain of Shechem, between Mounts Gerizim and Ebal, became a sanctuary of Jehovah, and there beneath an oak Joshua set up an oracular stone pillar, at a ceremony attended by the 12 tribes, as a witness to the Law (Joshua 24).

Shechem, the place of Law, and Shiloh, where the Ark was enshrined, became the chief sanctuaries and meeting-places for the amphictyonic league. United only by their religion, with no chief ruler or central administration, the 12 tribes lived as simple farmers and herdsmen in villages within their allotted boundaries. Justice was administered locally by clan and tribal elders. The question of boundaries seems to have been the most important subject discussed at the league meetings, for much of the Book of Joshua has to do with the various holdings of the tribes, their border marks and the sanctuaries or cities of refuge within their territories. Different schemes of sacred geography, generally based on the number 12, seem to have been applied, and in Joshua 18 is described a 7-part division of the land from the tabernacle of the Ark at Shiloh.

When faced with common danger, the 12 tribes had no recognized procedure for acting together, but times of crisis produced 'judges', popular leaders who were inspired by Jehovah to proclaim a holy war. This situation lasted for about two hundred years, from the end of the thirteenth century BC when the Israelite settlement of the Holy Land was complete, up to the Philistine conquest. The invaders stole the Ark from Shiloh, thus destroying the focus of the 12 tribes, and their amphictyony was threatened with dissolution. They were saved by the Prophet Samuel, a former priest of Shiloh, who became their religious leader and who strictly maintained the tribal laws and rituals. One of their fundamental traditions was of tribal self-government with no central monarchy. When the people clamoured for a king to lead them against the Philistines, Samuel at first reproved them, spelling out in alarming detail (I Samuel 8: 11–18) what a king is like and what he does ('He will take your daughters to be confectionaries, and to be cooks...he will take your fields, and your vineyards...he will take the tenth of your seed...he will take the tenth of your sheep...'). Nevertheless, a king was needed and cried out for, and Samuel therefore anointed Saul.

The problems in ruling as king over a traditionally anti-monarchist people eventually proved too much for Saul. He effectively smote the Philistines, but then his character disintegrated, he committed sacrilege and atrocities, and finally he summoned up from the spirit world the Prophet Samuel, who told him that he had lost favour with Jehovah and must now die. The following day, the Israelites were defeated in battle with the Philistines, Saul's three sons were killed and he committed suicide.

The reign of Saul, and that of David who succeeded him, marked a radical change in the character of the Israelite amphictyony. From being a religious congress of 12 independent tribes, it took the first step in the direction of becoming a national state. A monarchy requires a capital, where a court of officials can exercise the kingly functions which Samuel warned about. When David became king, he seized Jerusalem from the Jebusites and set up his capital there. The Ark was brought to Jerusalem from its previous, rustic shrine, but, though David built himself a fine palace with court offices, no temple was constructed. Evidently the old tradition still held firm, that the Ark should remain portable and be lodged in a simple, temporary shelter as a reminder of the heroic days in the wilderness.

Traditionalist scruples were overcome, and the Jerusalem Temple was built in the reign which followed David's, that of Solomon. Placed within it, on the Rock of Foundation enclosed by the Holy of Holies, the Ark served as the talisman of kingly rule. The former symbol of the constitution, the amphictyonic wheel, was replaced by the royal crown.

The legends of Solomon's golden reign identify it as the great age of Israel's civilized culture and prosperity. Through the developed arts of priestcraft, society was reformed on the traditional cosmic model. Solomon appointed a court of 12 nobles, whose names and family lands are listed in I Kings 4. Their astrological character is evident in that each of them had to supply the court with provisions for one month in the year. Solomon exemplified the philosopher-king, whose rule, said Plato, is the best that can be achieved once the paradise of innocent, nomadic life has been lost. Under Solomon music and literature flourished, priestly rituals within the cosmically proportioned temple spread the holy energy of the Ark throughout the country, and peace and happiness prevailed. 'At that time, Judah and Israel were many, as the sand which is by the sea in multitude, eating and drinking and making merry.'

With the death of Solomon the enchantment was broken and the 12-tribe union fell apart. The ten northern tribes separated themselves from Judah, Benjamin and those of the Levites who occupied Jerusalem, and two hundred years later, in 722 BC, they were carried into exile by the Assyrians. As the ten lost tribes they have ever since haunted history. Imaginative scholars have located them in every continent, and millennial theories which have been woven around them have influenced the course of modern Zionism. Judah and Benjamin, now restored to the Holy Land, await the return of their ten lost brethren. No one knows where they will appear from or how they will be identified, but the promise of their reassembly is given several times in the Old Testament, notably in Ezekiel 37: 21–22, in which it is said:

I will take the children of Israel from among the heathen, whither they be gone, and will gather them on every side, and bring them unto their own land: And I will make them one nation in the land upon the mountains of Israel; and one king shall be king to them all.

GEOMANCY IN THE HOLY LAND

From the beginning of the 2160-year period known as the Age of Pisces, the land of Israel became the Holy Land for Christians throughout the world. In the churches and chapels of all five continents, people sing hymns to Zion and speak of Jerusalem as their spiritual home. This accords with the astrological chart (figure 56) which shows Jerusalem at the centre of the Piscean sector, making it the destined holy city of that age. It also became a holy city of the Muslims. The Jews, meanwhile, have kept their minds and hopes fixed upon Jerusalem. Towards the end of the Age of Pisces they returned there and conquered it, thus fulfilling the first part of their prophecy, which continues with the reappearance of the ten lost tribes, the rebuilding of the Temple and the restoration of divinely inspired governance as in the days of King Solomon.

The small country which has generated such powerful mythology must clearly possess certain natural qualities which make it a centre of spiritual influence. We have suggested in previous chapters that every religion has recognized the same oracular centres and the lines of prophetic energy which run between them, and found it important to possess them. Throughout our era, the Holy Land and its sacred places have been fought over endlessly. Behind the apparent religious and political reasons for these wars is an underlying cause, the spiritual nature of the land itself. *63*

The northern gateway to the Holy Land is between the parallel ridges of Mount Lebanon and Mount Hermon, which shield like two crescent moons the fertile valley which traditionally begins at Dan. Between these crescents is born the River Jordan. It winds its way south along a deep geological rift, feeding three progessively

Fig. 61. A peak of Mount Sinai depicted by David Roberts, above the ancient monastery of St Katherine.

larger lakes, the Waters of Merom below the Golan Heights, the Sea of Galilee and the Dead Sea. Its fertile valley is wedged between the desert wilderness to the east and, on the west, the spinal ridge of the mountains of Judaea. Streams flowing into it from both sides form the branches of the Jordan's Tree of Life.

The end of the valley and its mountain rim is marked by Beersheba, the traditional southern limit of the Holy Land. Beyond it to the south, the mountain dragon rises again, and its tail is at Mount Sinai near the southern tip of the Sinai peninsula. The eye of the dragon is at Jacob's Well, about thirty miles north of Jerusalem. Here we find the geomantic centre of the Holy Land. It is sheltered by a ridge with two peaks, Mount Gerizim which is called the navel of the Holy Land, and Mount Ebal which is halfway between Dan and Beersheba. From here the two horns of the mountain dragon reach northwards, one to Mount Gilboa near Armageddon, the other along the ridge of Mount Carmel to the

61

sea. They mark the southern border of Galilee, and opposite them is the head of the northern mountain dragon, which curves along the far side of the Jordan, enclosing its left bank in a wing of high, desert wilderness. In the symbolic language of geomancy, Galilee is the pearl between the heads of two dragons. Its centre is at Nazareth.

THE AXIS OF VISION

Through the eye of the Holy Land and along its central spine and watershed runs a corridor of visionary places, comparable in many ways to the St Michael-Apollo alignment across Europe. Both are apparently based on a natural phenomenon, a vein of earth energy which inspires visions and oracles. As the European alignment links the best-known sanctuaries of the Archangel and the principal ancient oracle sites, the line through the Holy Land is remarkable for containing virtually all the places of vision mentioned in both Testaments of the Bible.

On this Axis of Vision appeared the Star of Bethlehem and the *62* glowing figures seen by the Apostles at the Transfiguration of Jesus upon Mount Tabor. It passes through Bethel, where Joseph had his dream of angels, and through the sanctuaries of Jerusalem, Shiloh and Shechem. The tribes of Israel approached the land of Canaan along the Axis of Vision from the mountain of revelation at Sinai. The southern part of this line coincides with the Way of the Patriarchs, the ancient pilgrimage route between the religious centres of the Holy Land. Abraham passed along it when he first entered Canaan and went through Bethel on his way to Egypt (Genesis 12:8). Jacob took the same path through Bethel to Bethlehem (Genesis 35: 1–20). Its northern extension from Bethel to the places of festival at Shiloh and Shechem is mentioned in Judges 21: 19, and Jesus proceeded along it from Jacob's Well up into Galilee (John 4: 43).

These mystical alignments have clearly been influential on the history of religion, but their discovery is recent and little is yet known about them. For those who are interested in their study, further notes on Israel's Axis of Vision are given below.

It begins at the southern peak of the Sinai peninsula, where the tail of the mountain dragon dips into the sea. This area is now a wilderness, but nature has endowed it with certain qualities which

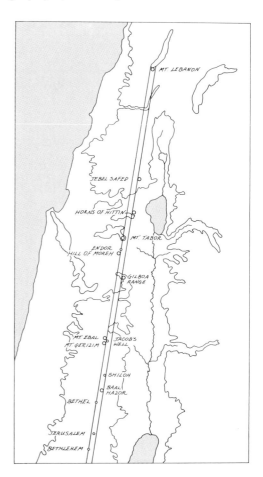

Fig. 62. The corridor through the Holy Land which includes most of the great sanctuaries and places of vision mentioned in the Old and New Testaments.

Opposite: *Fig. 63.* In this interpretation of the natural geomancy of the Holy Land, the mountain ranges can be seen as dragons, or sources of sacred energy, and the River Jordan as the Tree of Life. The prominent mountains in the range to the west of the Jordan are aligned with the sanctuaries to create the Axis of Vision through the Holy Land.

make it one of the earth's great sanctuaries. Its mountains are sharp and high, and the clear light emphasizes the pinks and greys of their granite folds. In pagan times the country was fertile and wooded, and up to the Middle Ages there were still groves and gardens among the Sinai rocks. Over thousands of years, deforestation and the encroachment of sand have made it a desert.

The eponymous god of Mount Sinai was Sin, a lunar deity, who was said to have received tablets of Law from the primal goddess, Tiamat. His shrines were in caves, and his sacrificial fires burned on the mountain tops. Many of the Sinai peaks are associated with visions and miraculous legends. Mount Horeb, of uncertain location, is named in Exodus 3 as the place of the Burning Bush, where Moses was instructed to deliver the Israelites from Egyptian

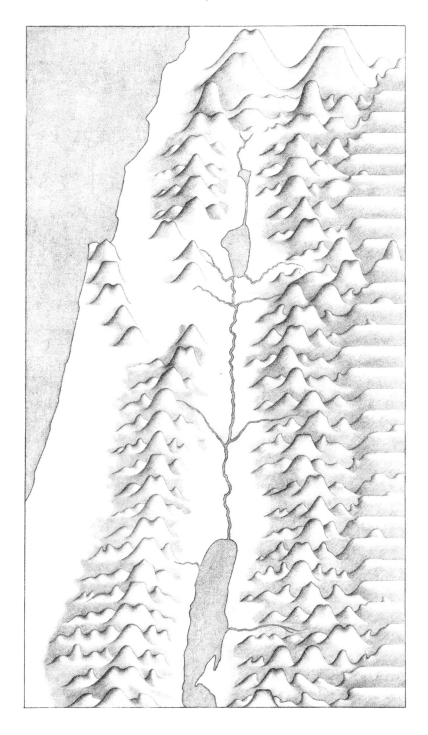

bondage. The Mountain of the Law, which the Old Testament identifies as Mount Sinai, is said in Elohistic texts to have been Mount Horeb. Modern belief equates Mount Sinai with Jebel Musa, a peak bounded by geological faults with a staircase of 2700 steps leading to its summit. Horeb is said to be Jebel Sirbal, an isolated, flat-topped crag 6800 feet high.

Next to Mount Sinai is Nebi Harun, where Aaron set up the Golden Calf, and between these two lies one of Christianity's most sacred mountains, dedicated to St Katherine of Alexandria. The story goes that, after her martyrdom, angels carried her body to the highest of Sinai's peaks, where it was found by monks from the nearby monastery of the Burning Bush. The monastery was dedicated to St Katherine in the ninth century and became a famous place of pilgrimage. Her relics are preserved there, and from her hand was obtained the miraculous, fragrant oil which travellers took back to Europe. In succession to Athena, St Katherine became the patron of philosophers, craftsmen and mariners, as well as the special protector of unmarried women. Her chapels are often on hilltops overlooking the sea, in imitation of Mount Sinai. In southern England, they used to be visited on her feast day, 25 November, by girls in search of husbands, and they were also beacons for pilgrim vessels. Voyagers to the Holy Land set their course by St Katherine's star, Canopus in the constellation of Argo.

Northwards from the peninsula of Sinai, following the route of the Israelites through the wildernesses of Paran and Zin, the Line of Vision runs parallel to the great rift along the Gulf of Akaba and enters the Promised Land. At Bethlehem it meets and merges with the Way of the Patriarchs. Three famous births have made Bethlehem the mother city of Israel. Benjamin, the last and most beloved of Jacob's sons, was born there, and on the northern outskirts of the town is the tomb of his mother, Rachel. The tomb is still venerated by Jews, Muslims and Christians, and it is a place of resort for women who want to bear children.

At Bethlehem was born a shepherd boy, David, the youngest of the sons of Jesse, and there he was recognized by the Prophet Samuel as the future king of Israel. A thousand years later, another descendant of Jesse, also known as a shepherd, was born in a grotto on the hill of Bethlehem. This event, coinciding with the dawn of the Age of Pisces, was marked by a strange star in the heavens. It was observed by eastern astrologers, and three magi appeared in Jerusalem, seeking the place of the notable birth which the star portended. Prophecies that a future king of Israel would be born in Bethlehem, and the guidance of the heavenly light, brought them to the birthplace of Jesus. The account is given in Matthew 2, and in Luke 2 is the story of angels appearing to shepherds to announce the nativity of Christ in the city of David.

The Romans made the natal cave of Jesus into a shrine of Adonis, but its Christian legend endured, and in 326 the first Church of the Nativity was built over the site. It was rebuilt in magnificent style in the sixth century, and has ever since been the holiest shrine of Christianity. A church of St Katherine stands beside it on the site of an old Crusader church, and nearby is the Milk Grotto where Mary nursed the infant Jesus. The soft, white chalk of its walls produces, when diluted with water, a milky liquid which is said to be beneficial to nursing mothers. A phial of it was preserved during the Middle Ages at England's leading sanctuary of the Virgin Mary, Walsingham in Norfolk, and the pilgrims' path leading to it was known as the Milky Way.

Jerusalem, five miles north of Bethlehem, is the next place in line on the Axis of Vision. Soon after his birth, according to St Luke, Jesus was carried up there to be presented at the Temple. The name of Jerusalem means peace and fulfilment, and a sacred quality in the light there seems to justify its reputation as the potential centre of an earthly paradise. Yet it is also a place of constant tension. Many nations have coveted it, and it has been seized at different times by Babylonians, Persians, Greeks, Egyptians, Turks, Hasmoneans, Parthians, Romans, Christian Crusaders, Saracens, Palestinians and Israelis. Solomon's Temple was destroyed by King Nebuchadnezzar of Babylon in the sixth century BC. Subsequent events include the building of the Second Temple in the time of Darius the Persian, its desecration in the second century BC when it was converted to a shrine of Dionysos, and its final destruction by the Romans, who placed a temple to Jupiter on the Temple Mount. There in 691 was erected the most beautiful of Jerusalem's sacred buildings, the Muslim Dome of the Rock, protecting that rocky outcrop whose legends declare it to be the centre of the world.

The Axis of Vision continues along the old highway to Bethel. As the central sanctuary of the twelve tribes of Israel, this place was long the rival of Jerusalem. The Ark of the Covenant was for a while enshrined there, and it was a great place of festivals and tribal ceremonies. The exact site of the ancient sanctuary is unknown, but it was not far from the highway and probably within the mile-wide strip which approximately defines the Axis of Vision.

The famous visionary episode which took place at Bethel was Jacob's dream, described in Genesis 28. He came there at nightfall, and slept in the open air with a stone for his pillow. In his dream he saw a ladder set up from earth to heaven, with angels ascending and descending upon it, an image which has been compared with the notes of a musical scale. From the top of the ladder, God told Jacob that the land was given to him and his descendants, who would multiply 'as the dust of the earth'. He then foretold the dispersal of the twelve tribes to all quarters of the earth, and their eventual return to the land of their fathers.

When Jacob awoke he realized that he had been sleeping on a holy spot. 'How dreadful is this place! This is none other but the house of God, and this is the gate of heaven.' He took the stone which had served him as a pillow, set it upright and anointed it as a memorial. Both the stone and the prophetic dream have influenced modern history. According to legend, Jacob's pillow was taken to Egypt and thence, by way of Spain, to Ireland. There it became the oracular coronation stone of Tara on which, for about a thousand years, the kings of Ireland were crowned. During the fifth century AD it was captured by the Scots and became the coronation stone of their monarchy. Edward I seized it in 1296, and it is now lodged below the Coronation Chair in Westminster Abbey. Mystical ideas associated with it have stimulated English support for the restoration of the Jews to Palestine. It is a strange story, but sacred rocks have always been influential in the affairs of the Holy Land.

Past Baal-Hazor, a high mountain once sacred to Baal and an Israelite place of observation, the Way of the Patriarchs goes up to Shiloh. The Ark of the Covenant rested there for the first two hundred years after the Israelites entered Canaan. Shiloh was one of their most holy places, a centre of pilgrimage and the scene of a great annual festival, referred to in Judges 21: 19, where maidens danced in the vineyards. After the Philistines carried off the Ark, it declined in national importance, but remained the tribal centre for Ephraim and Benjamin.

The way beyond Shiloh leads to Jacob's Well and the area which forms the geomantic centre of the Holy Land. The well, where Jacob and his children drank, lies on the eastern side of the ancient sanctuary of Shechem. Altars were raised there by both Abraham and Jacob, and above it are the twin peaks of Mounts Gerizim and Ebal. Beyond them, as one approaches from the south, is seen the snow-covered cone of Mount Hermon at the northern end of the Axis of Vision, floating like a white island on the horizon. In Judges 9 it is implied that Shechem and Mount Gerizim were symbolic centre points. In verse 6, Abimelech is made king 'by the plain of the pillar that was in Shechem', and in verse 37 people are seen coming down the mountain 'by the middle of the land', while others approach Shechem 'along by the plain of Meonenim'. The Hebrew word translated as 'middle' is *tabbur*, which also means a navel or omphalos, and Meonenim is a place name which, like Mediolanum, Meath and Meon, was applied to the central region of a country.

The Samaritans, a Jewish sect indigenous to Samaria, acknowledge Shechem rather than Jerusalem as the holy city, and Mount Gerizim is their symbolic world centre. On top of Gerizim is their *64* ancient temple, built to the same plan as the Temple at Jerusalem, and there also is their Rock of Foundation, the first thing that God created.

Jesus made Jacob's Well the centre of his mission to the Samaritans, as described in John 4. While walking northwards from Judaea towards Galilee, he rested by the well and asked a local Samaritan woman to draw him some water. She was surprised *65* at being addressed by an Orthodox Jew, whereupon Jesus declared himself to be Christ the Messiah, and promised her the spiritual water of everlasting life. The woman raised the question which divided the Jews and the Samaritans, whether God should be worshipped on Mount Gerizim or on the Temple Mount at Jerusalem. Jesus replied that God is a spirit, dwelling neither at Jerusalem nor on the Samaritans' mountain, and that he should be worshipped 'in spirit and in truth'. He then continued up the Axis of Vision into Galilee.

By way of Mount Gilboa and the Hill of Moreh or Little Mount Hermon, the line reaches the village of Endor. There are many caves there, one of them containing an ever-flowing spring, perhaps the Fountain of Dor, which gave the village its name. It was

Figs. 64–66. Three of the sacred places on the Axis of Vision. Above: the sacred rock on Mount Gerizim. Below: George Richmond's 1828 painting entitled *Christ and the Woman of Samaria* at Jacob's Well. Opposite: Mount Tabor, the site of Jesus's Transfiguration, as seen by J.A. La Trobe in 1838.

evidently a place of necromancy, for in I Samuel 28 is the story of how Saul, distraught and God-forsaken, went there to consult a wise woman. Saul had previously persecuted witches and spirit-raisers, and the woman was practising her art in secret, but she was persuaded to invoke the spirit of the Prophet Samuel, who rebuked Saul and foretold his death.

Mount Tabor, or *Tabbur* the middle point, is the next place of vision. High and rounded, billowing up from a plain, it is a prominent landmark. Streams flowing around it make it almost an island sanctuary. Tabor marked the boundary between the northern and southern tribes of Israel, and it continued as a place of tribal assembly long after the end of the Jewish monarchy. Its power has been much used by prophets and leaders. The Prophetess Deborah summoned the armies of Zebulon and Naphthali to Tabor before their victory over Sisera and the Canaanites. In earlier times it was a high place of Baal. Christians revere Tabor as the traditional place of Jesus's transfiguration, of which two similar accounts are given in Matthew 17 and Mark 9. With three disciples Jesus ascended the mountain, 'and was transfigured before them: and his face did shine as the sun, and his raiment was white as the light'. The spirits of Moses and Elias appeared, and the

66

163

disciples saw Jesus conversing with them. They were struck with awe, and Peter cried out that they should build tabernacles on the holy spot. As he spoke, a bright cloud overshadowed them, and a voice from it said, 'This is my beloved Son, in whom I am well pleased; hear ye him.' On the way down from the mountain, Jesus told the disciples not to speak about the vision until he had risen from the dead.

On its way through Galilee to the northern gateway of the Holy Land, the straight path follows the boundary between Zebulon and Naphthali, passing by two other places of religious note. Just to the east of it are the Horns of Hittin, a volcanic mount where certain traditions locate Jesus's Sermon on the Mount and his Feeding of the Multitude. Below it took place one of the decisive battles in history, when Saladin and his Saracens trapped the Crusader army against a cliff, kept them sweltering all day, armoured, in the face of the sun, and slaughtered them in the evening. So ended the Crusaders' reign in the Holy land.

The other site near the Axis of Vision is Jebel Safed. Set on a former beacon hill where the new moon was observed, Safed became during the Middle Ages a famous centre of Jewish mystical scholarship. The line touches the western edge of its mountain range and finally reaches Mount Lebanon. Much praised in the Old Testament for its beauty and fertility, this northern mountain was a source of timber for the ancient Egyptians, and from it came the great cedar trees which were used in the building of Solomon's Temple.

Jerusalem's Messianic ley

A remarkable and important discovery, recently published, concerns the position and shape of the former Temple at Jerusalem. Solomon's Temple was destroyed in 586 BC, and seventy years later the Second Temple was built in its place by the tribes of Judah and Benjamin on their return from Babylonian captivity. Herod began its elaborate reconstruction in about 20 BC, and his work was only just finished in 70 AD when the Temple was finally demolished by the Romans. Even the place where it stood was forgotten and for a long time it remained a mystery. The site was known to have been on the Temple Mount, but the best efforts of scholars and archaeologists had previously failed to locate it.

It had commonly been assumed that the Rock of Foundation, where the Ark stood in Solomon's Temple, was identical to the sacred rock beneath the Muslims' golden Dome. That is the traditional spot where Abraham bound Isaac for sacrifice, and a hoof-shaped indentation in its surface marks the place where Mohammed flew up to heaven on his winged horse, al-Burak. The fact that the same rock was claimed as central to their respective religions by both Jews and Muslims was an embarrassment and a potential source of conflict.

In 1974 Dr Asher Kaufman, a professor of physics at the University of Jerusalem, and his wife, both of British origin, began studying the Bible in memory of their daughter who had recently died. The problem of the Temple was in Kaufman's mind, and in Ezekiel 8: 16 he came across the first clue to its solution. The verse tells how the prophet, being shown the Temple at Jerusalem in a vision, saw 'about five and twenty men, with their backs towards the temple of the Lord, and their faces toward the east; and they worshipped the sun toward the east'. That implies that the axis of the Temple was orientated east-west, facing the Mount of Olives to the east.

The next clue was found in Numbers 19, where is described the ritual sacrifice of the red heifer, which took place on the Mount of Olives. Verse 4 says that the priest must sprinkle the blood of the heifer 'directly before the tabernacle of the congregation seven times'. Further details are given in the Mishnah, a collection of old Jewish texts describing laws and customs during the period of the Second Temple and subsequently. It records that the walls of the Temple were all high, except the wall to the east, which was lower 'so that the priest who burnt the red heifer might, while standing on the Mount of Olives, by directing his gaze carefully, see the entrance of the Hekal [the Sanctuary] at the time of the sprinkling of the blood'. The place of sacrifice must therefore have been on the eastward extension of the Temple's axis, near the summit of the Mount of Olives. By further study of records, archaeological relics and the topography of the site, Kaufman was able to identify approximately the place of the red heifer, to fix the line of the Temple's axis and, later, to discover the original ground plan of the building.

The Temple was not, as had been feared, on the site of the Dome of Rock but beyond it, on the northern edge of the Temple

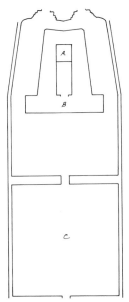

Fig. 67. The outline and principal features in the Jerusalem Temple from Kaufman's reconstruction.

A The Holy of Holies containing the Dome of Spirits.
B The main Temple sanctuary, the Hekal.
C The eastern Court of Women.

Opposite: *Fig. 68.* The Dome of the Spirits, covering the rock which was once contained in the Holy of Holies of Solomon's Temple, with, behind it, the Dome of the Rock.

67   platform. When Kaufman matched his reconstructed plan of the Temple with the modern site plan, he was amazed to find that an existing structure stood within the space he had allotted to the Holy of Holies. It is a Moorish canopy, sheltering an exposed
68   outcrop of rock known as the Dome of the Spirits or Dome of the Tablets. The latter name refers to a legend that the two Tablets of the Covenant once rested there, as they did upon the rock within the Holy of Holies. The obvious deduction, says Kaufman, is that this rock is the original foundation stone of Solomon's Temple.

Kaufman had read Alfred Watkins's book, *The Old Straight Track*, published in 1925, the first major work on 'leys' or straight alignments of ancient, sacred sites. Watkins attributed a mystical quality to leys, thus frightening archaeologists away from investigating his evidence. Yet the principle of sacred alignments is now generally accepted, and it is strikingly demonstrated by the alignment which coincides with the axis of the First Temple.

From the summit of the Mount of Olives, near a rock bearing a mark which Christians and Muslims take to be Jesus's footprint, the line goes through the eastern wall of the Temple area at the
69   southern end of the Golden Gate. This venerable structure, believed to be on the foundations of a gate built by Solomon, has been

sealed up for hundreds of years, ever since the Saracen conquest of Jerusalem in 1187, because of the disturbing legends and prophecies associated with it. The Jews expect that, when the future Messiah comes to Jerusalem, he will enter through the Golden Gate. Christians believe the same of Jesus at his Second Coming, for he has already passed through the Golden Gate, on Palm Sunday, when he rode into Jerusalem from the Mount of Olives on an ass. Those legends are the reason why the Muslims have blocked the gate; and they have gone further by planting a graveyard in front of it, intending to bar the way to a Jewish Messiah. In fact, the blocking of the Golden Gate seems to have been a tradition far earlier than Mohammedan times, for Ezekiel (44: 1–3) records it:

Then he brought me back the way of the gate of the outward sanctuary which looketh toward the east; and it was shut.

Then said the Lord unto me; This gate shall be shut, it shall not be opened, and no man shall enter in by it; because the Lord, the God of Israel, hath entered in by it, therefore it shall be shut.

It is for the prince; the prince, he shall sit in it to eat bread before the Lord; he shall enter by the way of the porch of that gate, and shall go out by the way of the same.

Fig. 69. A view of Jerusalem from the Mount of Olives to the east. The two blocked doorways of the Golden Gate are near the centre of the outer wall. The top of Absalom's Tomb rises to the left of centre. This prominent marker is shown more fully on page 175 *(fig. 73)*.

A Jewish belief is that, when the Temple was destroyed, the *Shechinah*, the Divine Presence which inhabited the Holy of Holies, left the city through the Golden Gate, and that when the Temple is rebuilt she will return along that same path.

Most interesting is the Muslim legend of the Golden Gate. It says that on the Day of Judgment the angel Gabriel will sound three blasts on a ram's horn to announce the Resurrection. All the peoples of the world will assemble on the Mount of Olives, where Abraham, Moses, Jesus and Mohammed will stand beside the scales of justice. After the judgment, the souls of those who have been rewarded with eternal life will pass over a bridge, as thin as a hair, as sharp as a sword and as black as night, stretching from the summit of the Mount to the Golden Gate.

This tradition of a mystical pathway from the Mount of Olives to the eastern gate into the Temple precinct has parallels in many other parts of the world. Throughout China and the East, South America, ancient Europe and wherever animistic religion has endowed the landscape with spirits, are records and relics of sacred paths, marked by straight alignments of shrines and monuments. Their legends identify them as spirit paths, channels of the earth's vital currents and the spirits of the dead. An example which has similarities with the line through Jerusalem is the system of aligned sacred places, linked by straight paths called *ceques*, which ran directly to a gold-lined chamber in the temple of the Sun at Cuzco, the state capital of the Incas in Peru.

As so far described, Asher Kaufman's alignment follows the traditional route of the Messiah from the top of the Mount of Olives, across the valley which separates it from Jerusalem, into the city through the Golden Gate, along the axis of the former Temple and over the Dome of the Spirits rock which was once enclosed within the Holy of Holies. Investigated further, the course of this straight line leads into a deep mystery. In 1987, after a visit to Dr Kaufman in Jerusalem, Christopher Gibbs pencilled the line on a street map of the city and extended it further west. The striking result was confirmed and published that same year by Dr Freeman-Grenville. He showed that the 'Messianic ley' from the Mount of Olives and along the Temple axis points directly to the most sacred rock of Christendom, the hill of Golgotha or Calvary whereon Jesus was crucified.

Golgotha is a natural rock pinnacle, a miniature sacred mountain, which in the time of Jesus stood just outside the city walls. There is archaeological evidence that it was once a place of pagan worship. It is traditionally claimed that Adam's skull is buried beneath it, and this contributes to its Christian reputation as the symbolic world centre.

About 35 yards north-west of Golgotha is the site of the cave where Jesus was entombed. It was enshrined in 335 beneath the rotunda of the Emperor Constantine's Church of the Holy Sepulchre. At that time Golgotha, surmounted by a cross, stood in the open air in a corner of the inner courtyard. When the Crusaders rebuilt the Holy Sepulchre in the twelfth century, the rock was contained within the church and enclosed by chapels. Today it is entirely hidden by masonry, apart from a small section of its summit, where Jesus's cross stood, which can be seen below the altar of an upstairs chapel.

The alignment thus links two of the world's most sacred rocks, Golgotha, the central symbol of Christianity, and the Jews' Rock of Foundation as identified by Kaufman. Moreover, it marks the

70

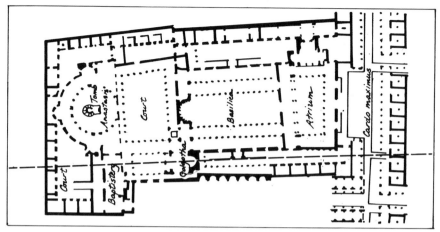

Fig. 70. Plan of the Church of the Holy Sepulchre as built by Constantine in the fourth century AD. Its main entrance was from the *cardo maximus* at the east end. The course of the Messianic ley to Golgotha is here marked along the aisle to the south.

main east-west axis of Jerusalem's northern quarters, and its eastern section follows the traditional pathway of the Messiah. This section is also the way by which some form of energizing power once entered the Temple through the eastern gate and penetrated into the Holy of Holies. In Ezekiel 43 the line is referred to as the way of the east. The prophet was taken in a vision to a gate east of the Temple, and

Behold, the glory of the God of Israel came from the way of the east: and his voice was like a noise of many waters: and the earth shined with his glory... And the glory of the Lord came into the house by way of the gate whose prospect is toward the east... and, behold, the glory of the Lord filled the house.

This description suggests that a flash of light entered the Holy of Holies, striking along the Messianic ley through the Golden Gate. An obvious interpretation is that the equinoctial sun, rising to the east from behind the Mount of Olives, cast a beam into the Temple's inner sanctuary and there created that luminous effect depicted in the words, 'the glory of the Lord filled the house'.

Yet the priestly operation which culminated in a holy light filling the Holy of Holies was not merely an effect of sunlight and shadow. The luminosity which entered the Temple was accompanied by a thundering sound, like a noise of many waters. In any case, because of the height of the Mount of Olives, the rays of sunrise would not have shone into the Temple through the Golden Gate but above it. Sunlight or moonlight may have contributed to the operation whereby the glory of the Lord filled the house, but it is plain from Ezekiel's account that other elements were involved.

The laws and legends of the Temple at Jerusalem depict it as the instrument of an elaborate sacred science which, because its method was to conjoin the two opposite, negative and positive, terrestrial and atmospheric powers in nature, is best described as alchemical. The alchemical *conjunctio* or sacred marriage took place in the Holy of Holies, the twenty-cubit cube made of special woods and metals which formed the heart of the Temple. Its walls and ceiling were lined with gold, and its floor in part was the Rock of Foundation. On the rock stood the Ark of the Covenant, and above it a pair of golden cherubim protected it with outstretched wings. They formed an energy circuit over the Ark, for two of the metal wings touched each other at the centre and the other two touched the walls on either side. Below the two inner wings of the cherubim and above the Ark hovered the *Shechinah*, the spirit of the land of Israel. The Holy of Holies was her marriage chamber, and there she awaited the seasonal visit of her mate, the shining, roaring apparition which streamed down the path from the Mount of Olives and entered her sanctum through the Golden Gate.

The visible result of that union was a glorious light emanating from the Holy of Holies. With it came a divine blessing upon the land and people of Israel. According to legend, the spirit of fertility raised at the Temple spread out through veins and fissures in the earth to all parts of the country. The sacred marriage may also have effected a meteorological change, an ionization of the atmosphere, for the Temple ritual evidently gave people a feeling of wellbeing. They were happy and prosperous, with high spirits, health and culture. That was in the days when the Temple stood. A relic of those days is the Messianic ley, the sacred pathway on the axis of the Temple. Along that path on a certain day the celestial bridegroom entered Jerusalem to meet his bride. There was light upon the Mount of Olives; a radiant pathway appeared across the valley and through the Golden Gate; the priests spilt blood, released spirit, made fire and smoke and raised their voices and trumpets; and a shaft, beam or bolt of great luminous intensity, concentrated perhaps by crystal lenses, struck along the Messianic ley into the gold-lined Holy of Holies where the energies of the earth spirit were most densely accumulated.

The function of the Temple, to marry the forces of heaven and earth for the benefit of human spirits and the fertility of the countryside, was exercised in connection with a highly technical, dangerous and unstable form of priestly science. Every detail in the ritual marriage ceremony had to be observed to the letter. Thus the appropriate sacrifices and burnings, the purifications, processions and chantings of the priests and the nature of their protective robes and regalia were strictly specified in Jewish Temple law. Many of these laws survive, but the esoteric knowledge behind the alchemical science of the Temple was lost with the Temple's destruction. Such knowledge, however, is never finally lost, and it has apparently been rediscovered on many occasions in history, in those numerous times and places where nations have been inspired to form 12-tribe, cosmologically ordered societies, attuned to divine law and blessings by the magical science of an initiated priesthood.

THE REVELATION OF THE TEMPLE

Further investigation of Asher Kaufman's Messianic ley through Jerusalem brings an astonishing revelation and also raises a great mystery. In the plan of Jerusalem's old streets and walls we find an overall pattern which sheds light on Biblical prophecies about the restoration of Solomon's Temple as the 'house of prayer for all nations'.

Jerusalem has been a walled town since at least 1800 BC, but the earliest evidence of a street plan is from the second century AD when it was captured, destroyed and rebuilt by the Romans. Its conqueror, Hadrian, designed the new city, using the methods of Roman geomancy as practised by the state augurs. They followed their usual procedure in city planning, first establishing an approximately north-south axis and making it the line of the principal street, the *cardo maximus*. Another street line, the *decumanus* running east-west, was drawn at right angles to it.

The augurs who redesigned Aelia Capitolina, the Roman name for Jerusalem, laid out its *cardo* and *decumanus* in accordance with the earlier city plan. The *decumanus* ran inside and parallel to an old city wall, the First Wall, and the line of the *cardo* followed that of the north-south Second Wall which was built

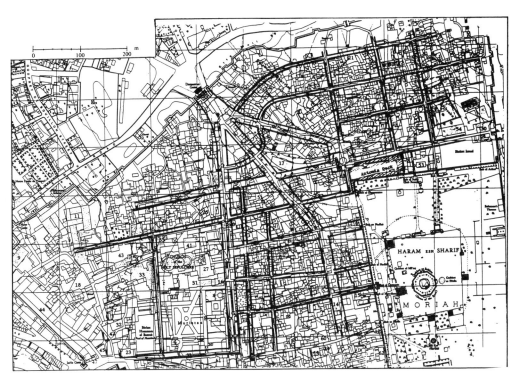

Fig. 71. Erich Cohn's reconstruction of the Roman street pattern of Jerusalem from the available archaeological evidence.

shortly before the time of Christ. Thus the old orientation of the city, parallel or at right angles to the Messianic ley, was preserved in the pattern of Roman streets.

Figure 72, an early twentieth-century map of the northern part of Jerusalem, shows the Messianic ley as the central broken line, running east-west and forming the main axis of the city. It passes from the summit of the Mount of Olives, through the Golden Gate, over the rock in the former Temple (the Dome of the Spirits) and on to the hill of Calvary or Golgotha in the Church of the Holy Sepulchre. It continues to the western tip of the old city walls.

Parallel to the Messianic ley, to the south of it, is shown an alignment which coincides in part with the line of the old First Wall bordering the Roman *decumanus*. Its western terminus is marked by the projecting corner of the ancient tower at the Jaffa

71
72

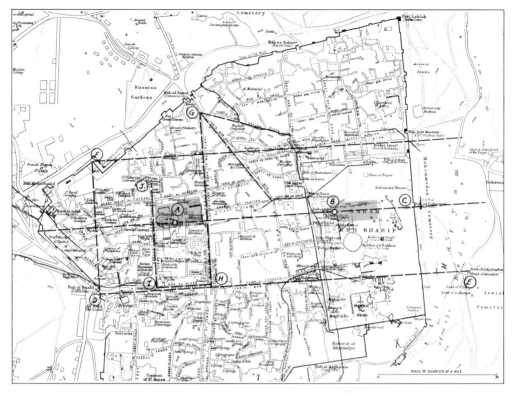

Fig. 72. In this map of Jerusalem's northern quarters, the Messianic ley is shown by the line along the centre of the diagram. It passes from the Mount of Olives to the west, through the Golden Gate (C), along the axis of the former Temple, over the Dome of the Spirits and on to the Rock of Golgotha. Street lines and landmarks contributing to the esoteric plan of Jerusalem include:

A Golgotha (ringed) in the precinct of Constantine's fourth-century Church of the Holy Sepulchre (shaded).

B The Dome of the Spirits (ringed) now identified as the Rock of Foundation in the Holy of Holies of the rediscovered Temple of Solomon (shaded).

C The Golden Gate.

D Corner of the tower at the Jaffa Gate.

E Absalom's Tomb.

F Corner of ancient city wall.

G Site of Hadrian's Column.

G-H *Cardo maximus.*

H-I *Decumanus.*

I-J Christian street.

174

Fig. 73. The Tomb of Absalom in the Valley of Jehoshaphat.

Gate, and its eastward extension is aligned upon Absalom's Tomb,   *73*
a rock-cut monument of the first century BC which replaced an
earlier pillar commemorating King David's favourite son.

Also parallel to the Messianic ley, and at the same distance from
it to the north, another straight line is indicated, running from a
prominent angle of the city wall on its north-west side and along
the edge of the Pool of Bethesda to the east. Above the Pool of
Bethesda its course is at a slightly different angle from that of the
Roman road from St Stephen's Gate to the old Forum.

The *cardo maximus*, which is still Jerusalem's main market
street, called Khan al-Zait Street, runs precisely at right angles to
the Messianic ley, as also does the eastern city wall to the north
of the Golden Gate. Other streets with the same orientation are
marked on the map (figure 72). This orientation is particularly
common in the Christian Quarter, the area bounded by the *cardo
maximus* to the east and the *decumanus* to the south. Elsewhere
in the city, the streets are mostly set at a different angle, tilted
slightly north of east, as exemplified by the two main stretches of
the Via Dolorosa.

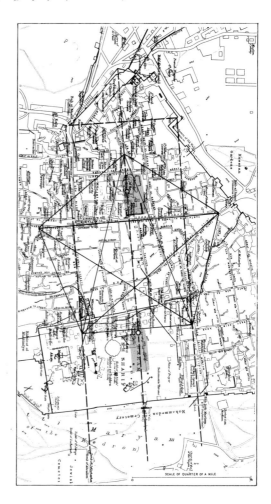

Fig. 74. The most obvious figure in Jerusalem's sacred geometry is the pentagon centered on the Messianic ley. Three of its lines are marked by streets of the Roman period or earlier, and its eastern side defines the west end of the former Temple.

Just inside the northern gate of the city, the Damascus Gate, Hadrian erected a tall column at the point where the *cardo* joined another important Roman thoroughfare, Tariq al-Wad or Valley Street. Also converging on that same point is the line of a third Roman street, Tariq as Sheikh Rihan, formerly a main thoroughfare leading into the Forum. The two angles formed by the meeting of these three streets are both 36 degrees, and in that is the clue to Jerusalem's esoteric pattern and meaning; for 36 and 72 degrees are the characteristic angles of the pentagram, the five-pointed star.

74   In figure 74, the map is turned so that west is at the top and east at the bottom, thus displaying the symmetry of the five-pointed star within a pentagon which develops from the old street pattern

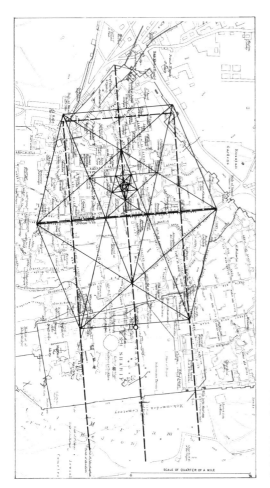

Fig. 75. The reciprocal pentagon is added to create the figure described in the next illustration (*fig. 76*). The series of reducing pentagrams within the upper pentagon shows that its exact centre lies upon the Rock of Golgotha.

of Jerusalem. The axis of the pentagram is formed by the Messianic ley, and its upper arm lies on the *cardo maximus*. The lower, eastern side of the pentagon is contained between the two parallel alignments flanking the Messianic ley. Its length is estimated at 720 cubits, the measure of the traditional Egyptian and Jewish cubit being 1.728 feet (0.527 metres).

The clue to the further development of this figure lies in the position of Golgotha within the pentagonal design. As shown in figure 75, it is located at the exact centre of the reciprocal pentagram to the first. The 'heads' of the two pentagrams overlap each other, and both have their upper arms upon the *cardo maximus*. In the symbolism of geometry this head-to-head union of two equal

75

177

pentagrams represents harmony between homogenous polar opposites, as in ideal marriage.

This lovely pentagonal scheme, forming a six-sided, equilateral figure, provides the framework of the symbolic design which Hadrian's Roman augurs planned or, more probably, renewed over Jerusalem. There is evidence of other geometrical patterns linked to it and to the walls and streets of the old city. Possibly the full scheme was a synthesis of all geometric types, hexagons, heptagons, octagons and so on, to create a geometer's image of 76 the universe. Most clearly indicated is the hexagon containing the two interlaced triangles of Solomon's Seal.

According to Kaufman, the outer width of the Temple was 208 feet (63.4 metres), and its length along the axis was 497 feet (151.6 metres). Expressed in terms of the previously defined cubit of 1.728 feet (0.527 metres), these measures are: width: 120 cubits; length: 288 cubits. The width of the Temple was therefore precisely one sixth of 720 cubits, the side measure of all the figures in the scheme of geometry.

This fact leads inevitably to a most delightful conclusion. In the course of reconstructing the esoteric geometry behind Jerusalem's city plan, we have discovered a rectangle which is six times the width of the former Temple upon the rectangle's axis. If the width of the rectangle is six times that of the Temple, perhaps it is also six times greater than the Temple in length. Its length in that case would be $288 \times 6 = 1728$ cubits. The value of the cubit is 1.728 feet, and if the length of the rectangle is 1728 cubits, the duodecimal framework of the whole scheme is made perfect; for 1728 is equal to 12^3, and so the length of the rectangle is a thousandth part of $12 \times 12 \times 12 \times 12 \times 12 \times 12$ feet.

We now realize that Jerusalem's northern quarters have been laid out by esoteric art as an image of a vast temple. The model for the work was the Temple of Solomon.

77 In figure 77 Kaufman's plan of the Temple, enlarged six-fold, is placed within the rectangle of the Jerusalem geometry, and the city's hidden aspect is immediately made plain. Jerusalem itself is the Temple. The Church of the Holy Sepulchre, containing Golgotha and the traditional tomb of Jesus, appears within the sanctuary of the Hekal, the front of which is set back from the *cardo maximus*, leaving room for marble steps in front of it, as in Solomon's Temple.

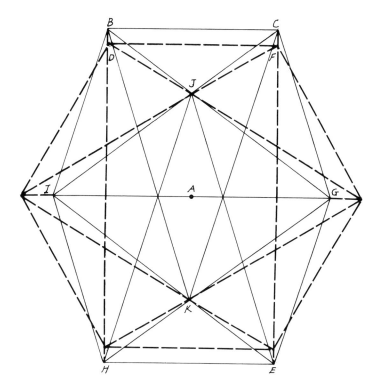

Fig. 76. The symbolic geometry of Jerusalem is made up of two symmetrically related figures. The first, illustrated upon the map in *fig. 75*, is the double pentagon (shown in solid line above). It consists of two interlaced pentagons, BCGKI and JIHEG. The complete figure, BCGEHI, has six sides and forms a 'squashed' or elongated hexagon.

The other figure is the regular hexagon (broken lines). The length of its side is the same as that of the pentagon. One of its sides, DF, is marked by the same letters on the plan of Jerusalem (*fig. 72*). The central point of the diagram, A, is the spot where the Messianic ley intersects the *cardo maximus*. G is the site of Hadrian's Column.

It will be seen from this diagram that lines drawn between the angles of the hexagon and also between the angles of the two pentagons almost come together at points J and K, and this provides a near solution to one of the classic problems of geometry: how to construct a pentagon with a side of equal length to that of a given hexagon. The method, by use of ruler and compass alone, is first to adjust the compass opening to equal the length of the side of the hexagon and, with centre at J or K, to draw arcs across the *cardo maximus*, thus finding points I and G. From I and G, further arcs are drawn to cut two of the extended diagonals of the hexagon at B, C, H and E.

Symbolized by this construction is the conjunction of two different elements, the organic (pentagonal) and the inorganic (hexagonal), or of soul and body. The union between the two pentagons signifies the marriage of two creatures of the same kind. This diagram is a symbol of the esoteric philosophy which constituted the wisdom of King Solomon.

The Temple was not, however, in the form of a perfect rectangle. From archaeological and other evidence, Kaufman has shown that it narrowed slightly at its western end, and that the Hekal was also tapered. The angle involved is the same as that by which the general orientation of Jerusalem's streets, such as the Holy Sepulchre Street to the north of the Church, parts of the Via Dolorosa and streets at right angles to these, deviates from that of the Messianic ley and the *cardo* and *decumanus* of Roman Jerusalem. The angle is about six degrees.

What is the age of this temple pattern over Jerusalem? When was it first conceived and who began the work of laying it down? Its most active promoter seems to have been Hadrian in the early part of the second century A D. Yet many essential features in the scheme existed before Hadrian's time. Jerusalem has often been destroyed, and its ancient streets lie up to twenty feet below the present level; but street lines are the most enduring part of a city, and Hadrian's replanning of Jerusalem's thoroughfares was largely based on a previous pattern. Its framework, the Messianic ley with the two parallel alignments, has an appearance of great antiquity. Our feeling is that the planning of Jerusalem as a symbolic temple goes back to its greatest period of glory, the reign of Solomon. The traditional wisdom of that great ruler is surely apparent in the beauty and power of the geometric construction which gives Jerusalem the permanent mark of a holy city.

There is good reason to suppose that the secret of the Messianic ley and of the esoteric geometry which forms the great temple over Jerusalem has always been known to certain people, perhaps until quite recent times. Constantine's architects, who demolished Hadrian's Temple of Venus and replaced it with the great Church of the Holy Sepulchre in 335, seem to have been aware of the Messianic ley, for they preserved its orientation in the aisle of the Basilica which led up to Golgotha (figure 70). The Messianic ley was undoubtedly recognized in 631, when the Emperor Heraclius brought back to Jerusalem the fragments of the True Cross which he had regained from the Persians. He carried the relics in a procession along its course, from the Mount of Olives, through the Golden Gate, along the axis of the former Temple and straight to Golgotha. There the Cross was enshrined, together with the cup from the Last Supper, the famous spear and other relics of the Crucifixion.

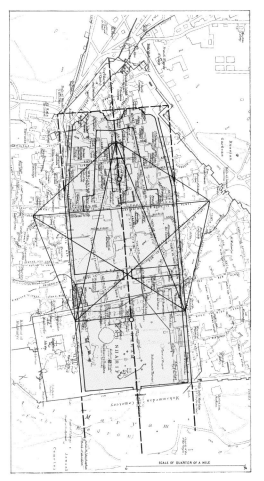

Fig. 77. The dimensions of the Jerusalem Temple, 288 × 120 cubits, are multiplied by 6, and the large-scale plan (shaded) fits exactly within the alignment system and basic geometry of the city. The east wall of the enlarged Temple coincides with the eastern wall of the city, and the Golden Gate forms the main entrance to the eastern Temple court. Golgotha and part of the Holy Sepulchre lie within the inner sanctum in front of the Holy of Holies. The front of the Inner Temple building, the Hekal, has its east part aligned on the *cardo maximus*. This is the prophesied Temple of Reconciliation whose appearance is linked with the fulfilment of Jerusalem's Messianic destiny.

The people most likely to have known the secret of the greater Jerusalem temple were the Knights Templar. In 1118 the first knights of this mysterious order appeared in Jerusalem and were immediately given extraordinary privileges. Ostensibly their purpose was to protect pilgrims on the roads to Jerusalem, but their real object was to reconstruct the Temple of Solomon, in other words to rediscover the secrets of the mystical Temple science which maintained the order and atmosphere of King Solomon's golden days. In this task they were supported by all the authorities of western Europe, secular and religious, who allowed them complete autonomy and freedom of action. During their sixty-nine years in Jerusalem the Knights made their headquarters in the al-Aqsa Mosque south of the Dome of the Rock, renaming it Solomon's Temple. The rites they conducted there were of a magical character, quite alien to Orthodox Christianity, and the ideal they pursued was far greater than the narrow ambitions of the ordinary Christian Crusaders. In their attempt to reassemble the ancient code of knowledge symbolized by Solomon's Temple, the Templar sages drew on the esoteric traditions of all three religions, Jewish, Christian and Muslim, and also on the traditions of paganism. Their intention was apparently to revive the ancient Mystery teachings in Jerusalem, so that worthy candidates of whatever religion might have access to initiation. Jerusalem was to be the greater temple of a new, divinely governed world order.

The mystical idealism of the Templars was rooted in the prophecies of all three religions, where Jerusalem is marked out as the location of a future earthly paradise. Over the actual city of Jerusalem hovers its archetype and model, the ideal city of heavenly Jerusalem. This perception passed into Christianity from Jewish mysticism, and it also shapes the way in which Islam regards the Holy City. Mohammed's first prayers were towards Jerusalem. Later he was inspired to make his prostrations to Mecca, and thus the axis linking the main Islamic monuments on Jerusalem's Temple Mount, including the Dome of the Rock and the al-Aqsa Mosque, points south in the direction of Mecca, at right angles to the Messianic ley. After Mecca and Medina, al-Kuds (the Islamic name for Jerusalem, meaning the Holy City) is the third most sacred place in the Muslim world. Yet at the same time it is distinguished above the other two as a place of vision, where heaven is nearest to earth, where Mohammed ascended to the Throne of Allah and where the Mahdi will pass through the Golden Gate along the Messianic ley.

The prophecy of Israel is that before the millennium the twelve tribes will regather at Jerusalem. At that time a new temple will be built. The importance of the temple is emphasized in Jewish commandments, most sternly in the Jerusalem Talmud: 'A generation which does not build the temple is accounted as if it had destroyed it.' Not surprisingly, therefore, Orthodox Jews are disposed to think literally about the task of rebuilding Solomon's Temple, on its former site and to its original proportions. Yet Isaiah makes it plain that the future Temple will not belong only to one people, but will admit 'the sons of the stranger'.

'For mine house shall be called an house of prayer for all people' (Isaiah 56: 7).

This vision of a universal temple, accessible to all who accept divine law and guidance, accords with the mystical view of Solomon's Temple as a symbol of the ancient wisdom rather than an actual building project. Moreover, in Revelation 21, where St John describes the heavenly city of New Jerusalem as it descends to earth, he says that no manmade temple is to be seen in it.

And I saw no temple therein: for the Lord God Almighty and the Lamb are the temple of it.

And the city had no need of the sun, neither of the moon, to shine in it: for the glory of God did lighten it, and the Lamb is the light thereof.

And the nations of them which are saved shall walk in the light of it: and the kings of the earth do bring their glory and honour into it.

And the gates of it shall not be shut at all by day: for there shall be no night there.

And they shall bring the glory and honour of the nations into it.

This surely is a reference to Jerusalem as one temple, acknowledged by the spiritually motivated in all nations and religions as a heavenly sanctuary on earth. That temple can scarcely be the exclusive property of any one of the three great religions which are centered upon Jerusalem; nor is it possible to divide it up among them, for the greater temple which lies across Jerusalem is indivisible, representing the harmonious union of all its parts. It is a symbol of that traditional philosophy and world-view, by which it is seen that every element in nature, every race and individual, has a legitimate place within a divine and potentially paradisial Creation. Jerusalem's greater temple is a revelation from the past which betokens further revelations and the fulfilment of prophecies. It appears to have been designed as the temple of a New Era and a new mode of religion, based on mystical perception rather than dogma, which transcends all present forms while enfolding and uplifting them all.

Bibliography

PART I

A. E. *The Candle of Vision*, 1920

Aristotle's Constitution of Athens (trans. T. J. Dymes), 1891

Bähr, Dr. K. C. *Symbolik des mosaischen Kultus*, 1837

Baring-Gould, S. *Further Reminiscences 1864–1894*, 1925

Caine, M. *The Glastonbury Zodiac*, 1978

Carley, J. *Glastonbury Abbey*, 1988

Cousins, Rev. W. E. *Malagasy Customs*, 1876

———. *Madagascar of Today*, 1895

Danielli, M. 'The State Concept of Imerina', *Folk-Lore*, LXI, No. 4, Dec. 1950

Daniel-Rops, H. *The Miracle of Iceland* (trans. Earl of Wicklow), 1959

Daumal, R. *Mount Analogue* (trans. R. Shattuck), 1974

Davidson, E. H. R. *Gods and Myths of Northern Europe*, 1964

Devereux, P. *Earth Lights*, 1982

D'Olivet, F. *Music Explained as Science and Art* (trans. J. Godwin), 1987

Du Chaillu, P. B. *The Viking Age*, 1889

Dumézil, G. *Tarpeia*, 1947

Dunraven, Earl of *Notes on Irish Architecture*, Vol. 1, 1875

Edda, Elder or Poetic (trans. O. Bray), 1908

Eliade, M. *Cosmos and History*, 1959

Epic of Gilgamesh, The (trans. N. K. Sandars), 1960

Ferguson, W. S. 'The Delian Amphictyony', *Classical Review*, Vol. XV, 1901

Freeman, E. A. *History of Federal Government in Greece and Italy*, 2nd ed. 1895

Geil, W. E. *The Sacred 5 of China*, 1926

Geldard, R. G. *The Traveler's Key to Ancient Greece*, 1989

Geoffrey of Monmouth *The History of the Kings of Britain* (trans. L. Thorpe), 1988

Gjerset, K. *History of Iceland*, 1922

Godwin, J. *Harmonies of Heaven and Earth*, 1987

Guénon, R. *The Lord of the World*, 1983

Guichard, X. *Eleusis Alésia* (trans. C. Rhone, 1985), 1936

Harrison, J. E. *Epilegomena to the Study of Greek Religion and Themis*, 1962

Heimberg, R. *Memories and Visions of Paradise*, 1989

Herodotus *The Histories* (trans. G. Rawlinson), 1964

High History of the Holy Graal (trans. S. Evans), 1898

Iolo Manuscripts (trans. T. Williams), 1848

Keary, A. & E. *The Heroes of Asgard*, 1930

Kenton, W. *Astrology*, 1974

Kircher, A. *Oedipus Aegyptiacus*, 1652

Larsen, J. A. O. *Greek Federal States*, 1968

Leatham, D. *Celtic Sunrise*, 1951

Le Plongeon, A. *Sacred Mysteries among the Mayans and the Quiches*, 1909

Le Roux, F. and C.-J. Guyonvarc'h *Les Druides*, 1986

Long, M. F. *The Secret Science Behind Miracles*, 1986

McClain, E. *The Pythagorean Plato*, 1978

Malory, Sir T. *Morte d'Arthur*, 1906

Maltwood, K. E. *A Guide to Glastonbury's Temple of the Stars*, 1964

———. *Air View Supplement to a Guide to Glastonbury's Temple of the Stars*, 1937

Maspero, G. C. *Histoire ancienne des peuples de l'Orient*, 1909

Matthews, W. H. *Mazes and Labyrinths*, 1970

Miller, Rev. O. D. *Har-Moad or the Mountain of the Assembly*, 1892

Pallotino, M. *Die Etrusker*, 1965

Palsson, E. *Celtic Christianity in Pagan Iceland*, 1985

———. *The Dome of Heaven*, 1982

———. *The Roots of Icelandic Culture*, 1986

Perry, W. J. *The Children of the Sun*, 1927

Plato, *Complete Works* (trans. H. N. Fowler, W. R. M. Lamb & R. G. Bury), 1914–29

Raleigh, Sir W. *The History of the World*, 1614

Rees, A. & B. *Celtic Heritage*, 1961

Rees, W. *An Historical Atlas of Wales*, 1959

Scherman, K. *Iceland: Daughter of Fire*, 1976

Scullard, H. H. *The Etruscan Cities and Rome*, 1967

Scully, V. *The Earth, the Temple and the Gods*, 1962

Sibree, J. *Madagascar and its People*, 1870

———. *Madagascar Before the Conquest*, 1896

Skinner, S. *The Living Earth Manual of Feng-Shui*, 1982

Snelling, J. *The Sacred Mountain*, 1983

Soothill, W. E. *The Hall of Light*, 1951

Strabo *Geography* (trans. H. L. Jones), 1960

Sturluson, S. *Edda, Prose* (trans. J. I. Young), 1954

William of Malmesbury *The History of Glastonbury* (trans. J. Scott), 1981

Williams, Rev. J. *A General History of the County of Radnor*, 1905

PART II

Bazin, G. *Le Mont Saint-Michel*, 1978

Broadhurst, P. *Secret Shrines*, 1988

Burrow, E. J. *Ancient Earthworks and Camps of Somerset*, 1924

Butler, S. *Alps and Sanctuaries*, 1890

Comte, L. *Le Puy-en-Velay*, 1986

Devereux, P. *Earth Lights Revelation*, 1989

———. *Places of Power*, 1990

Fletcher, Canon J. R. and J. D. Stephen *Short History of St. Michael's Mount Cornwall*, 1951

Lavelle, D. *Skellig, Island Outpost of Europe*, 1981

Michell, J. *City of Revelation*, 1972

———. *The Dimensions of Paradise*, 1988

———. *The New View Over Atlantis*, 1983

Miller, H. and P. Broadhurst, *The Sun and the Serpent*, 1989

Pole, W. T. 'The Archangel Michael: His Story', *Michael, Prince of Heaven*, 1951

Reynolds-Ball *Unknown Italy*, 1927

Richer, J. *Delphes, Délos et Cumes*, 1970

———. *Géographie sacrée dans le monde romain*, 1985

———. *Géographie sacrée du monde grec*, 1983

Richer, L. 'La Situation des lieux mystiques', *Aurores*, No. 22, April 1982

———. 'L'Axe de Saint-Michel et d'Apollon', *Atlantis*, No. 293, May–June 1977

Rojdestvensky, O. *Le Culte de Saint-Michel et le moyen age latin*, 1922

Rosenberg, A. *Michael und der Drache Urgestalten von Licht und Finsternis*, 1956

Stukeley, W. *Abury Described*, 1743

Taylor, Rev. T. *Saint Michael's Mount*, 1932

Thornley, M. 'One Pilgrim's Story', *Michael, Prince of Heaven*, 1951

PART III

Bergmeier, R. 'Jerusalem, du Hochgebaute Stadt', *Zeitschrift für die Neutestamentliche Wissenschaft*, Vol. 75, 1–2, 1984

Bezzant, R. and R. P. Pridham, *The Promise of Ezekiel's City*, 1952

Bouché-Leclerq, A. *L' Astrologie grecque*, 1899

Bright, J. *A History of Israel*, 1974

Chambers, H. E. 'Ancient Amphictyonies, Sic et Non', *Scripture in Context II*, 1983

Charles, R. H. *A Critical and Exegetical Commentary on the Revelation of St. John*, 1920

Cohn, E. W. *New Ideas about Jerusalem's Topography*, 1987

Cumont, F. 'La plus ancienne Géographie astrologique', *Klio*, Vol. 9, 1909

Drummond, Sir W. B. *The Oedipus Judaicus*, 1811

Dumbrell, W. J. 'Midian: A Land or a League?', *Vetus Testamentum*, Vol. 25, May 1975

Echenstein, L. *A History of Sinai*, 1921

Eliade, M. *The Sacred and the Profane*, 1959

Freeman-Grenville, G. S. P. 'The Basilica of the Holy Sepulchre', *Journal of the Royal Asiatic Society*, 1987

Geyser, A. S. 'Jesus, the Twelve and the Twelve Tribes in Matthew', *Essays on Jewish and Christian Apocalyptic*, Vol. 12, 1981

——. 'The Twelve Tribes in Revelation', *International Journal of Studiorum Novi Testamenti Societas*, Vol. 28, No. 3, July 1982

Godwin, J. *Athanasius Kircher*, 1979

Gonen, R. *Biblical Holy Places*, 1987

Guthrie, K. S. *The Pythagorean Sourcebook and Library*, 1987

Haenchen, E. *The Acts of the Apostles: A Commentary*, 1971

Hull, E. *Mount Seir, Sinai and Western Palestine*, 1885

Kaplan, A. *Jerusalem: The Eye of the Universe*, 1976

Kaufman, A. S. 'New Light on the Ancient Temple of Jerusalem', *Christian News in Israel*, XXVI, 1978

——. 'New Light upon Zion: the Plan and Precise Location of the Second Temple', *Ariel*, No. 43, 1977

——. 'Where the Ancient Temple of Israel Stood', *Biblical Archaeological Review*, March–April 1983

Landseer, J. *Sabaean Researches*, 1823

Lev, M. *The Traveler's Key to Jerusalem*, 1989

Packer, J. W. *Acts of the Apostles*, 1966

Peters, F. E. *Jerusalem*, 1985

Porter, J. L. *Through Samaria to Galilee and the Jordan*, 1889

Prag, K. *Blue Guide: Jerusalem*, 1989

Ptolemy *Tetrabiblos* (trans. J. M. Ashmand), 1917

Rahtjen, B. D. 'Philistine and Hebrew Amphictyonies', *JNES*, No. 24, 1965

——. 'The Philistine Amphictyony', *Abstracts International*, Vol. 25, 1964

Rogers, R. W. *The Religion of Babylonia and Assyria*, 1908

Smith, G. A. *Atlas of the Historical Geography of the Holy Land*, 1915

Stanley, A. P. *Sinai and Palestine in Connection with their History*, 1905

Strachan, G. *Christ and the Cosmos*, 1985

Thomson, W. M. *The Land and the Book*, 1863

Vilnay, Z. *Legends of Jerusalem: The Sacred Land*, Vol. 1, 1973

Watkins, A. *The Old Straight Track*, 1933

White, F. H. *Christ in the Tabernacle*, 1871

Sources of illustrations

1924.

50 Maps showing the exact bearing of the St Michael axis in England. Ordnance Survey, left to right: 1904, 1903–1906, 1901, 1900.

51 Glastonbury Tor. From a print, *c.* 1860.

52 The Cheesewring, Liskeard. From J. Blight *Ancient Crosses and other Antiquities in the East of Cornwall,* 1858.

54 Ground plan of Avebury. From W. Stukeley *Abury,* 1743.

57 Ruins of the temple of Artemis-Cybele. Drawing by Robert Travis.

58 The statue of Artemis at Ephesus.

61 Mount Sinai. From D. Roberts *The Holy Land,* Volume II, 1843.

64 The sacred rock on Mount Gerizim. From J. L. Porter *Through Samaria to Galilee and the Jordan,* 1889.

65 George Richmond *Christ and the Woman of Samaria,* 1828. Tate Gallery, London.

66 Mount Tabor. From J. A. La Trobe *Scripture Illustrations,* 1838.

67 The outline and principal features in the Jerusalem Temple. Reconstruction by Asher Kaufman.

68 The Dome of the Spirits and the Dome of the Rock, Jerusalem. Photo David Harris, Jerusalem.

69 Jerusalem from the Mount of Olives. From T. Scott *The Holy Bible,* 1844.

71 Reconstruction of the Roman street pattern, Jerusalem. Diagram by Erich Cohn.

72 Jerusalem's northern quarters. Map from G. A. Smith *Atlas of the Historical Geography of the Holy Land,* 1915.

73 The Tomb of Absalom. From W. H. Bartlett *Jerusalem Revisited,* 1855.

74 Map from G. A. Smith *Atlas of the Historical Geography of the Holy Land,* 1915.

75 Map from G. A. Smith *Atlas of the Historical Geography of the Holy Land,* 1915.

77 Map from G. A. Smith *Atlas of the Historical Geography of the Holy Land,* 1915.

The following illustrations are by courtesy of Christine Rhone: 3a–d, 4, 5, 6, 9, 13, 16a–b, 18a–c, 19, 20, 25, 26, 27, 29, 30, 32, 36, 48, 53, 55, 56, 59, 60, 62, 63, 70, 76.

Index